Space Chase

Book 3:

Daniel

By Dr Joe

Dedicated to:

Anyone who managed to read the series up to this point.

3,670,055

<u>Buy your own copy at www.DrJoe.id.au!</u>

More wonderful titles by Dr Joe & Creating Science:

Delightful high fantasy for the thoughtful young reader
Choice, set free
1: The Quest of the Tae'anaryn
2: The Tae'anaryn and the Wizard's Apprentice
3: The Tae'anaryn and the Paladin's Squire
4: The Tae'anaryn and the Enchantress's Chrysalis
5: The Tae'anaryn and the Spear of the Troll Prince

An engaging science fiction adventure that introduces real science concepts to readers.
Space Chase 1: Arrendrallendriania
Space Chase 2: Elizabeth
Space Chase 3: Daniel
Space Chase 4: The Mechanizer

Thrilling young adult science fantasy adventure.
The Dragon Riders of Pearl
The Dragon Riders of Pearl 2: Seven Worlds
The Dragon Riders of Pearl 3: Return of the Plague
The Dragon Riders of Pearl 4: Rage of the Dragonmen

And for the budding scientist:
Creating Science – Dr Joe's book of science experiments and activities
And
MaD science – The Managed Danger Project

Published by Creating Science by Dr Joe.
© Dr Joseph Ireland, 2015, 2019
All rights reserved. Reasonable portions of this work may be used for educative purposes.

National Library of Australia Cataloguing-in-Publication entry
Author: Ireland, Joe, author.
Title: Space Chase 3: Daniel
Series: Space Chase
Imprint: Creating Science
ISBN: 9780648494119
(Past edition: 978-1519781819)
Date: 25 Mar. 19
Pages: 248
Target Audience: Young adult / Primary school.
BISAC: EDU029030   Education, teaching materials
Dewey Number: F IRE
Lexile Number: 750

All characters appearing in this work are fictitious. Any resemblance to real persons, living or dead, is purely coincidental.

Do not attempt any activities or experiments in this book without competent adult supervision. Science is dangerous. And if you are suffering emotional distress such as but not limited to depression, anxiety, fear, paranoia, or hearing voices – see a professional.

Back cover illustration "Before the Escape" By Dr Joe.

Feedback and comments welcome – www.drjoe.id.au

Space Chase: Daniel

Table of contents

Table of images vi
Chapter 1 Best friends with an alien 1
Chapter 2 The competition 11
Chapter 3 Aliens among us 17
Chapter 4 Smorrom 28
Chapter 5 Failure 36
Chapter 6 Meditation 42
Chapter 7 Therapy 49
Chapter 8 Misery loves company 58
Chapter 9 Life 66
Chapter 10 The Lightning 75
Chapter 11 Robots 82
Chapter 12 The third assassin 88
Chapter 13 Class goes wild 97
Chapter 14 Nariou 106
Chapter 15 Confrontation 113
Chapter 16 End 120
Chapter 17 Daniel 127
Appendix 134
How to count in Coebri 135
About the author 139

Table of images

1 The three pronged widget - an impossible figure 1
2 The unwelcome visitor... 2
3 Techner circles. Which of the inner circles do you think is largest? 11
4 The Scintillating grid illusion, E. Lingelbach 1994. 28
5 Does this image have a spiral, or not? When is a spiral not a spiral? 36
6 The Herring Illusion, are the inside lines parallel or curved? 42
7 The love of recognising form when there is none – especially faces! 58
8 Square A is exactly the same shade of grey as Square B..................................... 66
9 As if the service spiders weren't useful enough - they also give free rides . 68
10 The floating finger.. 88
11 The Third Assassin 93
12 A different point of view 97
13 Alien spy orbs! 101
14 It ... moves.. 106
15 Dustbeast 121
16 The principle of closure. How many triangles are in this figure? 120

Chapter 1
Best Friends With An Alien

The three pronged widget - an impossible figure[1]

It wasn't easy being Chase.

First, his dad was crazy; filling their home with broken dreamcatchers and used incense sticks. He never seemed to get organised, and never cleaned the house. Of course, his mother was crazy too, but in the complete opposite direction. She worked twenty five hours a day and never came home. His brother was always getting into trouble and, let's not forget, his best friend was an alien.

Not just any alien either; she was a super advanced alien robot spaceship ... thing ... that everyone seemed

---

[1] Hi all! Dr Joe here, jovially elucidating the science throughout this amazing adventure via footnotes ☺ Each chapter in this book begins with an optical illusion for you to enjoy, and this one is the Blivet or 'devil's tuning fork'; an impossible figure of indeterminate origin. Try looking at it while covering one side, and then the other. It makes sense as a figure when you only see half of it, but becomes an impossible figure when you try to make sense of the whole object at once – what fun! It reminds us that observation is a very personal, and thus somewhat biased, experience. The way we *think* about the world has a big role in the way we *see* it. Fascinating!

to want. Some weren't too bad, like the dangerous Australian Federal agents who were now playing all nice to try and get her to share alien technology with them.

Then there were others, like the murderous alien pirates who kept on sending robot assassins after her, just like the robot assassin that was standing in front of him right now.

The unwelcome visitor...

They were walking home from school, the three of them: Chase, his twin brother Lucky, and their alien friend Arrendrallendriania, or Arren for short. The robot melted into their dimension and for a moment it just stood there. It had a weird metal box for a head/chest, with two clawed arms and four legs.

"Surrender your Class Two Research and Reclamation vessel," it ordered them in a mechanical voice. "It is coming with me."

"Aww great," Lucky complained. "Juuust what we need! You know, I actually felt like doing my homework for once today."

In reply it fired a plasma blast from its main eye that blasted into the ground just in front of him. One more step, and it wouldn't have been the concrete that was a smoking hole; it would have been Lucky's foot.

"Umm, options?" Chase asked Arren.

She looked nervous, like she normally expected to know when assassin robots would turn up. Today, however, it was apparent that she did not.

"Here's an option," Lucky grinned. Barely bending his knees he leapt off the ground and front-flipped up towards the robot. His foot smashed into its face, dinting it badly, and he landed on its knee and tried to yank out a robot arm.

Chase yelled out as another one of those arms swung around from behind the robot. The arm with a glowing knife blade. Lucky seemed to know it was coming without even looking, twisting away and swinging around, just in time to grab the third arm. He used it to gain his footing on the leg he started on.

"Let's even this up," He smirked. In the next instant, the knife had swung around and cut another arm right off. Standing on three legs the robot tried to kick him, but Lucky dodged and it ended up putting a robot foot right into its own chest.

Lucky laughed.

The robot spun violently right around at its hips, but Lucky jumped away, without a scratch on him.

"Are you all right?" Chase asked Lucky while the robot tried to disengage its own foot from the enormous hole in its chest.

"Better than ever," Lucky replied.

"Come on, we'd better get out of here." Arren insisted, pulling at their hands.

They ran, leaving their school bags right there.

"Where are we going?" Chase puffed, running out of breath far too soon.

Lucky hadn't even broken a sweat.

"We need to get back to the spaceship," she replied.

"I thought it was on Jupiter?" he asked. She'd mentioned that morning she was going to check out Jupiter, just for fun.

"That's why it's taking so long!" she huffed.

They ran to the old alley where they usually took a shortcut back home. To their dismay someone had blocked it off with a huge, professional looking, solid metal fence.

"Oh *great!*" Arren protested.

Lucky took two steps running up the wall, snatching the top edge with one hand and was standing on the two meter high fence as quick as Chase could think.

Arren was very strong; grabbing the top she pulled herself up in an instant.

Chase ran to the wall and tried banging on it to see if it was actually a gate, which he knew it wasn't.

"Chase, give us your hands!" Arren cried out.

He reached up, and they began to haul him up with unbelievable strength. Almost all the way over, however, there was the blast of red light and the tell-tale hum of a plasma blast. Lucky dropped him. Arren fell backwards and had to catch hold of the fence. Chase found himself lying painfully and quite vulnerable on top of it.

He turned around to see the robot, stumbling along on two legs. The other still intact arm carrying the broken one while trying to use its plasma gun on Lucky.

"You know, now I know why you gave us those super alien upgrades!" Lucky teased Arren. The robot fired several plasma blasts at him. Bright, hot, magnetically contained doses of super-heated material that would have put a hole in him in less than a second. Lucky somehow managed to dodge or dance out of the way of them all.

"It's not that!" Arren protested, "I just, umm …" She scrambled to try and help Chase cross the fence.

"Get a move on, boy!" Lucky told Chase, and in the midst of dodging a new plasma blast, managed to reach down, grab him by the seat of his pants, and fling him over the fence. Arren squealed, and Chase roared. He found himself flying through the air only to land painfully flat on his back two meters down on the other side of the fence.

"That hurt," he intended to say, but found he was so winded his lungs just didn't seem to want to work right now. All that came out was something like, "Weee, wheeem!"

"Not as much as if it catches us. Run, Chase!" Arren cried, starting to look genuinely worried.

Chase stumbled with Arren's help up the path, racing to get around the houses where the robot couldn't shoot them. Lucky stayed on the fence, jumping with supernatural precognition so that the robot couldn't even hit him. Then he turned to dance down another fence, dodging and jumping, and at one point doing so with a one armed hand stand. He'd caught up to them in a second.

He still hadn't even broken a sweat.

"What now?" he grinned, clearly enjoying himself.

Suddenly there was a screeching, exploding sound as the robot smashed its way through the metal fence.

"We need to get home," Arren replied.

Chase's side started to hurt, at least, more than his back. He discovered he was having trouble breathing. A *lot* of trouble. His head felt dizzy and Arren slipped under his arm. He held on tight. He wasn't sure if he was running or skipping while she carried him.

"Asthma?" she asked.

He could only nod.

"Let's get you home so you can breathe," Lucky said, now looking worried too.

They ran, but every step seemed harder and harder. Chase's head began to spin, and Arren was now all but literally carrying him. A few frantic paces later they were almost home.

"Too late," Arren said.

Chase turned around in time to see Lucky kick a paving stone from someone's garden with such force it flew up and into his hands. The robot fired again, twice more, but both times Lucky somehow seemed to catch the blow in the stone, which kept shattering away tiny pieces of itself.

A second later they were running through the door, the neighbour's brick wall giving them cover.

Chase held his ribs. He almost couldn't stand up.

"Just breathe," Arren told him.

"I'm trying!!" he screeched back at her. He was finding it quite hard to think sensibly while suffocating. He didn't need to be told to breathe; he was doing everything in his power right now to *just breathe*.

"OK," she told him, "Relax. Tell your body everything is fine, you can handle this. Think about something that calms you down."

Really, he only wanted to hit her. To hit *something*. Gasping for breath he desperately tried to relax. He thought about the beach. He liked the beach. And the sand. And the way the breeze was always cool.

Suddenly, he opened his eyes with surprise. He was breathing normally again.

"Wow. That was quick." Arren said, clearly impressed.

But they still had a problem. "We need to get out of here," he told them.

Lucky was riffling through the kitchen drawer for some kind of weapon.

"Come on!" Arren shouted.

They ran out to the backyard, filled with dozens and dozens of vibrant plants, particularly due to Lucky's strange new hobby of growing vegetables. Lucky kicked up another paving stone.

"We make our stand here?" Lucky asked.

Suddenly, there was a loud bang, and the sound of rockets firing. The next moment the badly smashed up robot jumped over the house and landed right in the middle of the garden. It had its plasma gun pointed only millimetres from Lucky's head.

"Surrender," it ordered.

Arren knelt down, and put her hands over her head, indicating they should do the same.

Chase was grateful for a rest, but still didn't know what to do. Arren had given Lucky some super alien upgrade; it was why he could dodge plasma blasts before he could even see them. She'd given him superpowers too, of the more subtle kind.

It was time to use them.

Chase tried to use some of the skills Arren had shown him. He tried setting the robot on fire, but nothing happened. He tried pushing its hand out of the way with his mind … nothing again.

Lucky was waiting, trying to reach for a planting stick as carefully as possible.

The robot ignored him. Then it opened up its badly dinted chest, and pulled out a little gem studded collar. It was pretty, but in a freaky kind of way. It seemed to radiate tyranny and fear. In that instant Chase realised it was a slave collar, and it was intended for Arren.

With all his feelings he tried to throw the collar far away into the bushes.

It barely budged. In fact, he wasn't even sure if it was him, or the robots naturally jerky movement, especially since it was carrying its own arm.

Then, without warning, a bathtub plummeted down from the sky. It smashed down and crushed the robot where it stood. The plasma blaster fired harmlessly into the ground, and then there was silence.

Chase looked up to see Arren's spaceship, partially see-through, floating above them in the air. A pair of service spiders were retreating from the landing platform where they appeared to have hoisted the old copper bathtub Arren had been fixing in her spare time.

"Arren, you busted your bathtub!" Lucky said.

"The robot would have noticed matter from any other world," she replied.

"You smashed it with a bath!" Lucky laughed. "Oh, that's so funny!"

He burst out laughing, and then so did she.

But Chase didn't feel like laughing as he looked at the broken robot, slowly disappearing as service spiders took him back into the dimension where Arren's spaceship usually hid.

He felt miserable.

He had been useless, *less* than useless! They would have been much safer and swifter if he hadn't been there to slow them down.

He just thought they were probably better off without him.

Chapter 2
The Competition

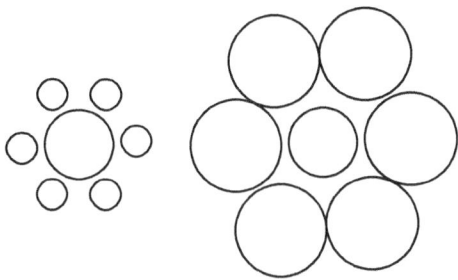

Techner circles. Which of the inner circles do you think is largest?[2]

Chase still felt a little sorry for himself the next day, but there was little time to think about it. They'd made it to school safely, and then through most of the day. Arren had sent her spaceship to search all over the planet, but it didn't find any evidence of alien assassins. It looked like they weren't coming back, at least not for now. So he decided to relax, forget about it until it happened again. He'd be ready next time.

He was glad they were in science class; science was his favourite. It seemed the teacher had realised he had some very competitive students in his class. And, being a teacher, he was going to use this.

"I have a new competition for you all," he announced, "as part of your assignment on scientific inquiry skills,

---

[2] Neither, they are exactly the same. But because of the influence of context our minds assume the circle on the left is larger: The smaller circles around it make it appear larger than the circle surrounded by larger ones!

you have a section on observation and inference. So what I'm going to do is hold a little competition to see who can come up with the most interesting optical illusion[3]. Winner gets a Mars bar!"

Everyone was silent.

Chase knew what they were thinking - why would a chocolate bar be worth competing over? Especially since they could all just buy one at the canteen if they wanted.

"So ..." a voice called from the back. It was Mark T, a class one bully. He was always trying to get one up on Chase and Lucky, and was just as often losing. But losing made him even angrier, and being angry made him more determined to win; even if it was nothing more important than a silly class assignment, "So ... there's going to be a winner?"

And that was the moment when Chase knew the competition was on. Once again, it would be him, his

---

[3] What is an optical illusion? It is the experience of seeing something as it isn't. Seeing is actually heavily influenced by our life experience and expectations. For example, when a hand is moving towards your face it appears to get larger. But you typically don't think it's *growing*, you have learned by experience that it is getting *closer*. But a baby probably can't tell the difference, and has to decide for themselves as they learn and grow. This is called the 'theory ladenness' of observation. Even *seeing* requires a *theory* of what is going on in the world!

It reminds me of a silly quote. Man 1: "Oh, look, a hippopotamus head sticking out of the river." Man 2, very seriously: "Actually, it's probably a whole hippopotamus, you just can't see the rest of it." (Once again, you know this, but at what age did you learn about perceptual constancy?)

twin brother, and their alien friend Arren versus Mark T and his two 'lackeys'.

"Yes. Now, get to work!"

Lucky pretended not to like school, but he was always there on time and almost always did his homework. Truthfully, his first love was sports, and he was always being picked first for teams.

And then there was Chase, who was always picked *last*.

"I've got a nice illusion," Arren interrupted his thoughts as the class began to get themselves organised for searching the internet for illusions to start their project. "How about our blind spot?"

Most of the students at school had decided that Arren wasn't really an exchange student: That information was either a misunderstanding or a deliberate rumour to hide the fact that she was really a refugee distantly related to Chase and Lucky. Like a cousin, only twelve times removed. A rumour went around that her father was a spy and was being held prisoner in Saudi Arabia, and she'd moved here to Australia for safety. Lucky just went on making rumours worse, while Arren just smiled and told everyone how happy she was to be here. Of course, the whole disappearance of Lucky and Chase's mother years ago made people wonder if the same thing with spies hadn't happened to them as well, but one look at their Dad would usually convince them otherwise.

"What's a 'blind spot'?" Lucky asked, not really paying attention while he checked his school email instead of getting ready.

Chase answered, "It's the spot in front of your eyes that you can't actually see. You have one in each eye."

"Really?" Lucky asked,

"Yes, you're blind in both eyes, just a touch."

Lucky said nothing, but looked at them like he didn't really believe it. "So why don't I see it?" he asked.

"Because your brain covers up the image," Arren explained. "It's how most optical illusions work. Your eyes present a picture to your brain, and your brain has to make sense of it. And in the process of making sense, it often has to take shortcuts, or it makes mistakes. There'd be no sense seeing a big dark patch, so the brain covers it up, usually using what the other eye can see so that you don't even notice."

Lucky just stared. "I don't think that'd count as an optical illusion," he protested.

"Yes it will!" Arren disagreed.

"Naw, look!" Lucky insisted, swivelling his chair over to Chase's computer where the screen was full of images. "That's what an optical illusion looks like. Not … things we can't even see."

"It *is* an optical illusion, Lucky," she insisted.

Chase didn't even want to be drawn into the debate, but just sat there, not really looking at illusions. His mind began to drift once more. He was thinking about assassin robots, and how useless he felt yesterday.

Suddenly Arren stopped talking, and turned around to look right at him. "You all right, Chase?"

Something in her voice must have worried Lucky, because he stopped too.

They just looked at him.

He sighed, "Just ... forget it."

They didn't. Instead, they sat there. Waiting.

He sighed. Two people he could *never* keep a secret from.

He leant forward, and whispered, "It's just, that robot yesterday. He could have killed us. You two were *so* amazing! I just ... I was just useless."

Lucky said nothing. Chase could tell he agreed, but would never admit it out loud.

Arren sat there. "You weren't useless Chase. I saw you trying to help. And if you hadn't run with us it would have used you as bribery to capture me."

"That's just my point!" Chase argued, feeling much more upset than he wanted to. "I was less than helpful! I didn't do anything! You've got these super powers Lucky, but what have I got? A calmer mind? A better perspective? How's *that* going to help us stay safe against ... against the Coebri?"

Lucky sighed.

Arren put a hand on his arm, "Don't discount your own abilities yet Chase. You may find you have more to offer than you believe."

He pushed away, looking blankly at the glowing screen. "So, what is my power?" he asked her.

Her mouth opened and closed, but she didn't seem to know what to say.

So Chase quoted her, his voice high pitched like a girl's, "the silver light is *very* individual, it will take time ..."

Lucky laughed at his attempt to copy her.

Chase sighed.

Arren reached over, and grabbed the pen out of his pocket. "Is this yours?" she asked.

"I guess," he replied. "Dad got a whole bunch of them at the start of the year."

"Yeah," Lucky said, "it's his. Seriously, Chase never loses them, and only gets a new one once the old one is well and truly dead. I don't know how he does it – maybe *that's* his super power!"

She smiled, and put the pen in her pocket.

Chase could almost *feel* the pen disappear into another dimension, "What do you need it for?" he asked.

"Oh, just a little project I've been working on, you'll see." she said with a wink, then said no more but began working on her assignment.

He looked at her, wondering why she was typing on a keyboard when it seemed she could just download the entire internet into her brain in seconds. What *was* she doing pretending to be a school girl? Why was she *really* here on Earth?

And how do you ask someone about that? he wondered.

Chapter 3
Aliens Among Us

A tactile illusion: If one hand is placed in cold water and the other in hot for a minute or so, and then both hands are placed in lukewarm water; the lukewarm water will feel hot to the hand previously in cold water, and cold to the hand previously in hot water.[4]

---

[4] In order to perceive things, your body often cannot use 'presence', but rather, 'change.' You know what happens when you stare – with the same image stuck on your retina for around 30 seconds, the nerves stop noticing any difference, so they stop firing, and you experience a kind of blindness until you move your eyes again. As a matter of fact, your eyes are constantly jiggling around to prevent an image disappearing – it's very hard to keep them still. Every sense we have works a little this way: Becoming dizzy is tricking the nerves in the semi-circular canals that movement in one direction is constantly happening. When you stop moving, the nerves are still firing, and you feel like you're spinning when you're not! Even a bad smell eventually seems to disappear because your nose cancels it out in order to notice new changes.

In the end Chase decided the most logical course of action would be to simply ask her. If the killer assassin robots came along again, it might be helpful to know. To be fair, he wasn't the same person since he'd met her and she'd soaked him inside gentle silver light. He was, what did she say 'empathic'. It was nice to know what people were feeling, really know, like he could see inside their brains or something. Sometimes it was like a word, or a picture, but somehow he just knew. It was fun. It worked with animals too, like helping them know what Arren's buddy Obi-jo the hyper intelligent orangutan wanted. But it didn't seem a very good way to help save the world.

Still, there was one person he simply couldn't read. His best friend, Arren.

"Arren," he said on their way home from school the next day, Lucky having gotten detention for misbehaviour again, "What is your story?"

She looked surprised, "Whatever do you mean Chase?"

"I mean, it's like my dad says. Everyone has a story, a reason they do the things they do, even if they don't make much sense. So, I'm wondering what your story is.'

She paused a bit before answering, "Because what I do doesn't make much sense?" she teased him.

"No!" he insisted, then realised he wasn't making any sense either. "I mean, well, yes. I mean, I hope you don't mind. Why do you pretend to be a human? Why do you spend all your time at school when you could be, you know, anywhere? Why... pretend to study just like everyone else."

She sighed, not seeming to know what to say, "I'm not really ready to tell you my story yet Chase."

Suddenly, Arren stopped walking, "Do you smell that?" she asked with her nose turned up.

A moment later Chase could smell it too; something had died in the nearby trees.

He looked over and found a very dead Indian myna bird.

"Indian myna," Arren said, "from India. Not native to Australia. Brought over in 1876 for recreational purposes, they – "

"Hey," Chase suddenly realised something, "I didn't know you had a sense of smell."

"Of course I have a sense of smell, I am a humaniform robot, after all."

"Yes, but smell?"

"I have all the five senses, thank you; sight, hearing, olfactory, kinaesthetic and balance."

"I thought they were sight, hearing, touch, smell and taste?" Chase asked.

"Who told you that?" Arren asked.

"Everyone," Chase replied.

"Well, have you ever wondered who came up with that list of five senses?"

"I don't know, never thought about it, really. Some scientist, I guess."

"Unlikely, no one knows who it was. Most blame Leonardo DaVinci. Italian in the 1700's, amazing guy. Painted the Mona Lisa. Around about his time they decided there were five senses, and it kind of stuck. But nowadays, with people challenging everything, some argue that the five traditional senses aren't the best way to organise how we sense the world. Some suggest we have five external senses, sight and sound, kinaesthetic for sensing where our body is and what it's doing, olfactory combines taste and smell since they are the same basic processes of detecting chemicals, and balance. Seriously, why isn't balance counted as one of the senses, Chase? It might be located in the inner ear, but it has nothing to do with the sense of hearing. Why, Chase? Why!?"

He held up his hands, and smiled at her enthusiasm. "I have no idea, Arren. You go fix things."

"I will! And you know, those are only the external senses. What about the internal ones? Blood sugar, tiredness, there's at least twenty of them. And what about detecting carbon dioxide levels in the blood?"

"We can do that?"

"Yes, though you experience it as the suffocation feeling. Too much CO_2 in your blood. Interesting fact here, your body can't actually tell when it's got too much or too little oxygen. You can suffocate to death and not even know simply by breathing too much of just about anything except CO_2."

"Scary," Chase said.

"Yes," she agreed. He liked how they had these informative conversations all the time.

"And there you go again," he complained, "telling me all this stuff, and then pretending you need to go to school!"

She sighed, her melancholy returning. If he didn't know any better, he'd think she just tried to distract him with science. Again. "Well … it's like this … I can feel other people's feelings too. Not like you though, not like it's all a part of me. But this body I have here is designed to assimilate the human experience. I'm 'researching' for want of a better word, trying to understand what it means to be human; to dream, to exist, to fear and to want. Everything about being a human is amazing to me, and I am trying to understand that. I *need* to understand it. When I'm in the classroom I can sense the blood flow in people's brains, I can record everything they say, and how they say it. I can process their voice prints and galvanic skin responses. But, I'm still not one of you Chase. I'm still not a person. You're … mysterious, miraculous, unfathomable! I have a few questions of my own too, when I can phrase them so they make sense. I guess that's… that's why I do it. I'm not studying science; I'm studying what it means to be 'people'."

"Oh," said Chase, really not sure what to say at all.

She hit him on his arm, playfully.

"That's it?!" she demanded.

"Oh, well, yeah. I mean, good luck with your research and all. I don't know what it means to be 'human' either."

She looked like she didn't believe him. "Like, whenever you mention your mother, Lucky's heart rate increases and he either changes the topic or wanders out the room – and it's like NOBODY NOTICES. Every time! What's with that? He loves his mother and wants to talk about her more than anyone I know, but then he doesn't want to. I simply don't get it. How is that even logical??"

Chase was stunned, and had no idea Lucky was doing that, and even less of an idea about what to say. But then he thought about his brother, and about conversations they'd had, and a thought struck him, "I guess… he's hurting. He's just avoiding a topic that still makes him want to cry."

"Oh," Arren said, very reverently. "I would have never thought of that, especially with his 'go and get 'em' attitude. Yes, I suppose it *is* logical now. That's what's so impressive about you humans. How do you do it? Everything you do makes sense, but it makes sense on a different level, every time."

Chase was silent. He had no idea what to say. Again. It seemed to be happening a lot recently.

"And Kassie has a crush on you," she suddenly announced.

"What?"

"Kassie, you know. I've been watching her. Her blood pressure rises, and the veins in her cheek dilate when she looks at you sometimes. I'm sure she doesn't even know yet. But I'm telling you because I don't want you to hurt her feelings, you know, be insensitive?"

"I … what?" Now he was feeling uncomfortable. Kassie, who had fainted at the sight of blood when someone cut their fingers with a pair of scissors in grade 3? He never even noticed her.

"Yes, Kassie, my *friend*. Be nice, Chase, she's a nice girl."

"I … don't think I want her to have a crush on me," he replied.

"You?" Arren said in a doubtful voice, "Who want nothing more than to be the centre of attention in class? There you go again, illogical, impressive, unintelligible human."

He shook his head. Centre of attention? He liked being right, and helping out the teachers, but it wasn't about getting all the attention. And now Arren declares Kassie has a… he decided to ignore this until it all went away. Seriously, it was way too soon for relationships!

Arren smiled, like she knew she was making him uncomfortable. "Shut up Chase," she hit him again. "Come on, I'll race you home."

And she took off.

She did not get far.

Three steps in, and she fell straight to the ground with a cry of surprise and pain.

Chase ran up to her immediately, "What is it?" he begged.

She rolled over, and there, crawling right up the outside of her jeans pants, was a little metal cockroach.

She squealed, "Get it off, get it off!"

Chase wondered why she didn't get it off herself, but after only a moment's hesitation, swept it away.

It landed about four meters away, rolled over, and began scurrying towards her again.

With inexcusable panic, she tried to crawl away from it.

Chase didn't know what the problem was, but gathering his courage, stomped the tiny robot into the ground. He could feel it wiggling under his school shoe, so hoping it wasn't indestructible, he ground down on it. There was a snap, a pop, and a small cloud of smoke began to rise.

"I got it," he said.

"I can't move my foot," Arren explained, not paying any attention. She seemed terrified.

"Arren, are you all right?" he asked, rushing to her side. He wished they hadn't let Lucky out of their sight.

"I can't move my foot, I can't move my foot," she kept repeating.

"They must have poisoned you as well, or something. You're not thinking straight. Come on Arren, snap out of it!"

She looked up at him, something in his words seeming to get through. She held out her arms and he pulled her to her feet.

"I'm getting us out-"

She began, but was interrupted by an enormous, and very unwelcome clang. Chase looked up, and saw the air about twenty meters away wavering with a strange, blue forcefield.

Arren stifled a scream, "They cut us off!"

He looked up then, and saw her spaceship just beyond that forcefield. But it wasn't able to get any closer to them, though it tried, glistening into their dimension continuously, and in a very obvious manner if anyone was looking to see what all the fuss was about.

"I can't," she muttered, and tried to collapse.

Chase wouldn't let her, "Come on Arren, we've gotten through worse! That bug must have some poison that's messing with your thinking. Let's just walk to the ship, we can do it!"

She looked up, her pupils dilated and her face full of confusion and fear, nothing like a moment ago. "Yes … cybertoxins. I can fix them in the ship. The forcefield won't stop us, we can walk." She took a few steps, and screamed again.

It was another bug.

Chase leapt on it in a second, and turning around, saw another three heading towards Arren at full speed.

With gallant determination she kept hopping towards the ship, while Chase ran around her smashing the new bugs. Some he got first time, but they were *tough*.

Then he saw them, hundreds of them, burrowing themselves out of the hillside and charging towards them.

"Run!" he told her.

"I can't," she whispered.

This was a real problem. If they got her here … if they pulled her apart.

The ground turned dark under the massing swarm.

"Chase," she muttered, "remember your training … they're metal."

He assumed she was referring to the time he'd helped repair her spaceship by telekinetically reshaping the metal. And if these bugs were metal.

He spread his hands, willing their metal joints to fuse together, and the hoard momentarily stopped.

Then they kept coming.

It wasn't working, again. He still wasn't strong enough.

In frustration he stomped on the nearest one, and it exploded like a firecracker under his shoe.

It was touch. Last time he'd been able to touch the metal.

But there were too many to take on at once.

"Chase!" Arren screamed. He turned, and it took his breath away. The bugs in front of him had merely been a distraction. There was a second hoard, and it had already found Arren. Her shoes were covered in bugs, and her legs, and her knees.

He didn't waste another moment. With a roar of anger he ran towards her, and picked her up off the ground. It must have been the adrenaline, because she felt very light. He ran, full speed. The bugs tried to trip him, but he just let them splash under his feet like water. They tried to bite his arms and legs, but he ignored the pain and just ran.

With only a few paces to go, the bugs began to pile up in a heap. They were trying to make it impossible for him to pass.

So with all his might, with one final, desperate lunge, Chase threw her. It was probably less than a meter, but it was enough. She landed outside the forcefield, and her spaceship grabbed her in an instant.

The bugs got away from him as fast as they could. They did not get far. He found the buried force field transmitter and smashed it with his foot. A moment later Arren's massive ship flew into the area and began viscously disintegrating them all.

They were safe again.

For now.

Chapter 4
Smorrom

Black dots appear in the corners between the squares, but only when you're not looking directly at them!! The Scintillating grid illusion, E. Lingelbach 1994.[5]

It took her a good three hours to recover, while Chase paced backwards and forwards outside the cupboard that lead to the dimension where she hid her spaceship. But eventually she invited him in.

---

[5] Based on The Hermann grid illusion by Ludimar Hermann in 1870. How does it work? We don't know! There are two competing theories; the Lateral inhibition (RGC) theory or the effect of S1 type simple cells in the visual cortex. Good luck visual scientists, let me know when you make up your minds!

Service spiders clattered around in a calm, almost relaxed manner helping her fix things for the next school market. They went past the garden where her friend Obe-Jo, the super-intelligent orangutan, was learning all about alien computer systems while relaxing under the light of Arren's spaceship's artificial indoor sun.

"Those bugs gave us a bit of a fright, didn't they Chase?"

"That they did, Arren."

"Looks like the Coebri are getting creative in their desperation." They were passing some workshops now, where if he didn't know any better, the machines within were preparing what looked like weapons.

"Well," she explained, "If it's a fight they're looking for, it's a fight they'll get!"

He nodded; glad she was getting ready to defend herself. Knowing her creativity, and vast alien knowledge, he sorely doubted the Coebri could ever come up with something that could stop her now!

Yet, he noted with some curiosity, they didn't head towards the control room where the screens were able to reveal a picture of anywhere on the planet. They went instead to the medical room, which left him wondering why.

"So ... " he offered, hoping she'd start explaining things.

But she didn't. She just smiled as the door slid open. Inside the room was a hive of activity. The medical bed, the one she'd used at least twice before to stay alive, was surrounded by service spiders of all sizes, all over the walls. The wires and tubes moved about as if alive, twisting and stretching while lights danced among the project they were focused on. Chase couldn't even see the bed for the mess of writhing activity.

"What are you doing?"

"Actually, we're done," she announced. She walked forward, and Chase followed, curiosity nagging him.

There, swirling on the medical bed, was a little cloud of black dust. It seemed unable to settle on a shape, spinning and twisting constantly. It was an orb, then a cylinder, then a strange pattern like spinning twine. And all the time the black dust moved and swirled.

"What is it?" Chase wondered.

"Something I made, using only materials from your house, Chase, so technically it'll always belong to you. I disintegrated your pen, a rock, and … I think there was a clock too, hmmm. Anyway, I changed them. Now, look closely, what do you see?"

He bent down to study the swirling dust. It looked like a mini tornado, only a touch more gentle. "It's amazing," he admitted.

"No, look closer. Look there!" She indicated towards the centre.

The dust formed an hourglass shape then. There, hidden right in the centre, was a single little crystal, like quartz.

"What is it?" Chase asked.

"Quartz," she laughed. "A computer, specially designed to interphase with human technology and physiology. That little crystal there could hold your entire internet several times over, and have room to spare."

"Wow," Chase said. "What do we need it for?"

"Simple. We need it for you."

"Really?"

She smiled, like she was really happy to be giving him something. "You seem a little uncertain about how you can help out. And you seem to need a little more help until you have the confidence to work your 'super powers' on your own. So, if you'll allow, if you let this little guy work with you, you can use it to enhance your psychokinetic abilities."

"Really?" Chase said, the excitement bubbling inside him.

"Really!"

Then, as he watched, the dust swirled up, and spun wildly around his wrist. He tried not to panic, it was such a strange sight. He wasn't sure if he was excited or nervous.

He voted for excited.

In a moment the dust settled together and formed an ornate, rustic bracelet. The quartz crystal settled on the outside looking like a nice, but somewhat tacky gem. It felt as solid as steel.

"Wow," Chase wondered. "What else can it do?"

"Well!" Arren announced, tossing her hair back with pride, "A lot! It can form into a phone, a GPS, a Wi-Fi satellite link with special anti-assassin robot technologies. But most especially, it has a little something for you."

"But," Chase said, a doubt nagging him from something she'd said a few weeks ago, "Aren't you worried about this technology falling into enemy hands?"

"I thought about that. This little crystal here controls and shapes the dust. It can make new specks at the rate of several million an hour. But any speck that becomes lost or stolen will become inert immediately. It will, effectively, burn itself out and become real dust right away. You could even eat it. Not that you should, it's just that it's not harmful to life, that's all I mean."

"You mean, it's a computer. An edible computer made from dust."

"Not edible!! But, yes, he's a computer," she smiled. A second later the dust swirled around his wrist and settled on the medical bed. In an instant it had reformed to become a perfect replica of an iPhone, complete with scratches.

"That is so –" Chase was about to say cool, when a sudden thought struck him. "Ah, Arren, you said 'he', does that mean that thing is … alive?"

"Of course!" she smiled.

He rubbed his wrist.

"Don't worry Chase. He's not *that* alive, but he will talk to you if you ask. Think of it as a kind of class *four* vessel."

"What's his name?"

She looked confused for a moment. "Well, I never really thought of that. But if you're wondering, his designation is Smorrom Tzup Driarnalla. It means four 512s and 47. I suppose that doesn't make much sense since the Coebri use a base sixty-four numbering system."

Chase's head was swimming. "Drian? Isn't that part of your name?"

"Yes, of course."

"I don't ... hang on, are you telling me that your name is really a number? Only a number!"

"I ... what's the matter Chase? What did you expect?" her voice sounded tense, but he hardly noticed.

"What does, what does you name mean?" he asked.

She frowned. "Arren means ... well ... 'fourteen'. But that's only a number Chase. When you say it, it's not 'just a number' anymore. Not to me."

But something did spin Chase out about it. "Arren means 14! Your name is 'fourteen'!"

"Stop *shouting* Chase!" she said, getting upset.

It stopped him, "Hey, sorry, I didn't mean you to get so worked up."

She turned to face her little bed. When she spoke it sounded like she was quite a bit upset. "I've been nothing but a number for a very long time, Chase. When I came here, when I met you, you and Lucky made everything different for me. I wasn't just a number anymore. I was someone's friend. Someone who was willing to protect me, and someone who gave me good advice. You made my name mean something, Chase. Please ... please don't ever take that away."

He fell silent. A part of him just felt awful. How could he have been so tactless? That wasn't like him.

But another part of him, a quiet part that he had never noticed before, a selfish part that seemed to want to remain hidden, *just didn't care.* Arren wasn't human, and if she ever forgot that, there could be trouble …

Chase shook his head violently – what was he thinking! Arren might not be human, but she still had a *soul*. She still needed friends. *Just didn't care?* That just wasn't like him.

He put his hand on her shoulder, "Sorry, Arren. Guess I just got carried away."

She turned, and blinked away her tears. He must have really hurt her. "That's OK," she smiled. "Here. You want to learn how to protect yourself, and me? Well, let's teach you how to throw around lightning!"

Then Chase smiled too.

***

Lightning practice was the most frustrating, annoying, enjoyable thing Chase had ever had to do.

"No, no, no!" Arren repeated, getting frustrated too now. "You're still trying to force it! There's enough electricity in the universe already, you only need to tell it where to go![6]"

"I'm trying!" Chase repeated. "But it keeps wanting to just zap towards whatever is lying about! Especially pointy things[7]."

They'd been trying for an hour, the little computer 'Smorrom'– he still needed to think of a better name

---

[6] Can people throw lightning? Science has no convincing evidence as yet, but there certainly have been some interesting claims!

[7] Yes. Yes it does.

than that – strapped around his head to form a psychokinetic headband that made throwing lightning easy, apparently. The robot kept on making little telepathic suggestions that appeared in his mind, but they made so little sense. Arren insisted he could throw lightning without the headband, but he still couldn't even manage a spark between his fingers without it.

Sparky fingers. Really impressive, and not going to do much against an assassin robot. He tried and tried to push the electricity out of him and towards the targets, but nothing he seemed to do could convince it to move where he wanted it. It was like trying to hold a wet, wiggly puppy while jumping on a trampoline covered with dishwashing detergent. It just wasn't going to happen.

Two hours later, Chase had had enough, "Arren, look, it's just not going to work today".

"Come on then Chase," Arren said, "let's go look for some more illusions!"

They walked out, Chase taking a quick look back at the almost surreal scene of peace and quiet in the indoor garden. Lopi the snake was basking on the trees, and Obi-Jo typing on some kind of alien keyboard with great glee. It was such a peaceful picture.

He really hoped it would never have to end.

Chapter 5
Failure

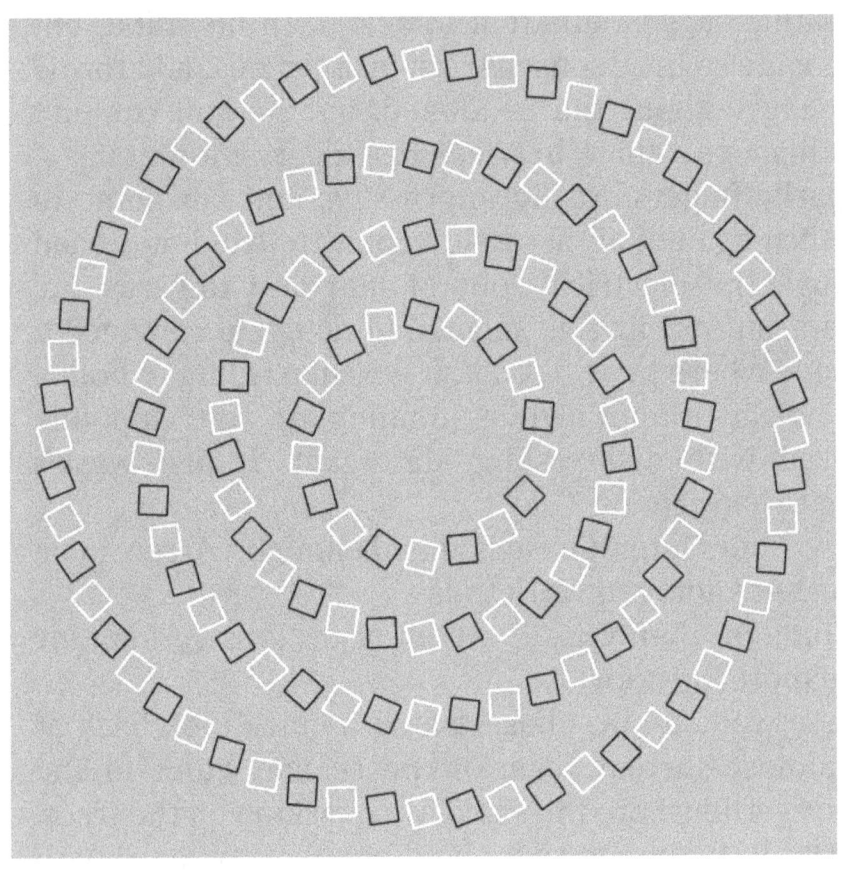

Does this image have a spiral, or not? When is a spiral not a spiral?[8]

---

[8] When it's Pinna's illusory intertwining effect by Jochen Burghardt, described in Pinna's illusory intertwining effect. Pinna, B., Gregory, R.L. (2002). "Shifts of Edges and Deformations of Patterns". *Perception* **31**: 1503-1508.

The next morning, Chase and Lucky were in their room, and Lucky looked impressed.

The little dust robot was shifting and floating all over the room. Every object it touched, it tried to imitate. It was being a scrunched up bit of paper, it was imitating the clock, it tried to copy the toy dinosaurs. Sometimes it didn't do a very good job, and would have to try again.

"That's so random," Lucky said.

"Actually, I think its name is Smorrom," Chase replied.

"S'moron? That's a dumb name," Lucky deliberately mispronounced. "Let's just call him Random."

Chase opened his mouth to disagree. Lucky was always naming things whatever he wanted, whether they wanted naming or not. But he had to agree, it was better than a number.

"Random." Chase pondered out loud. "Do you like that name? Is it better than being a number?"

The dust made a cyclone, and swirling over a pair of scissors tried to replicate them, but ended up with a pair of dinosaur legs instead of blades.

Lucky burst out laughing, "Yup, that's his name!"

Even Chase had to agree with that, but didn't say anything. The dust tried to form a stegosaurus properly again, and rearing up on its hind legs nodded at him.

Chase burst out laughing too.

Perhaps Random was a good name for it.

"Boys!" Dad called from the other end of the house, "Hurry up, you'll be late for school."

Lucky didn't bother changing, but Chase put on his favourite t-shirt. He picked up Random, who blew over to become a big fat wristwatch. It was black this time, much more fashionable than any previous attempt. Chase was pleased.

He laughed. This looked like it was going to be a good day.

***

But it wasn't. Something about failing to make lightning really upset Chase. The day just got worse and worse. He didn't speak to anyone. He didn't want to. Everyone was avoiding him. Even the teachers didn't try to speak to him.

They were in maths class, and he was picking the paint off his pencil. He was just so miserable! Arren sat by him, but said nothing. She was trying to explain fractions to Kassie again.

Fractions, like wasn't that year six maths? Was she stupid, or just too lazy to learn it back then? he thought, wondering dimly if he was just being mean again.

He must have said something, because Arren turned around and stared at him. He could feel Kassie worrying about him, feeling sorry for him. He didn't care.

He looked away.

Was he being spoilt? He didn't know. Having abilities beyond normal was pretty special. He *could* tell what people were feeling. But that was still pretty useless against assassin robots. As useless as little sparks. He could do them without Arren's little robot now, but it took at least ten minutes of solid concentration.

Useless.

He sighed, and tried to get back into the work. He looked up at the teacher. A teacher trying to teach them maths. Did he know how it felt to be useless? To face down an impossible adversary with an *asthma attack*? To watch your brother dance on one hand while dodging death dealing plasma blasts? To waste a whole day with an alien who could do anything she wanted, so she pretended to be a *schoolgirl!*

Suddenly the teacher stopped mid-sentence. Chase could sense something was wrong. The feelings whelmed up inside the teacher, stirring, crashing, overflowing.

"I'm sorry," the teacher muttered, removing his glasses to wipe his face, "I just … " and then he burst into tears, and ran out.

"What just happened?" Mark T shouted.

Nobody spoke, but Chase found it quite funny. Honestly, the teacher had just burst into tears because he was trying to teach *maths*!

A thought jolted his attention, and he turned to see Lucky staring meaningfully at him.

You did that, bro, he seemed to say.

Chase shook his head.

Lucky nodded, slowly.

Chase just grinned … then the smile slowly faded. *Did I?* He wondered.

***

They nailed him as soon as class was over, which, in hindsight, was pretty patient of them really.

Lucky and Arren marched alongside him, pressing against his shoulders so they could whisper.

"Dude, what were you doing to the teacher?" Lucky asked.

"What? Nothing!" Chase protested, but not sincerely, "I didn't do anything."

"Dude, you've been wallowing all morning. You've been dragging us all down! Now you, I don't know, you just broke our maths teacher, you know that."

"No, I ... I ... Arren?"

"Dumping. I've never seen it done like that before Chase. It's when a human dumps their bad moods on another person, forcing or tricking them into accepting their 'negative vibes' as your dad might say. I wondered what had happened."

"You think I did that?" he asked.

"You're an empath[9], Chase. You can sense other people's feelings, *and* you've the silver light empowerment. Worse yet, you're human. Dumping bad emotions onto other people is something you all do. Whenever you come home from school and start shouting at your parents, whenever you hurt yourself

---

[9] Just about everyone can judge the moods of other people, but some people claim to be so sensitive that they can actually feel other people's feelings. No scientific consensus exists if this ability is actually possible, but it makes for some great storytelling!

to get attention from others, you're dumping[10]. You're trying to make other people feel bad so that you don't have to."

Chase thought about that. "You think I sent my bad feelings to the teacher?" he asked.

They nodded.

"And, for whatever reason, the teacher accepted them." Arren explained.

Chase was aghast. This was serious. Not much for against a robotic assassin, but manipulating other people's emotions? That was serious ...

But at least it's something, he thought, and they went home.

---

[10] Yes, just about all of us dump our bad moods on others, dragging down those around us when we feel down. But this 'dumping' Arren is talking about is a little different. Can we telepathically force our unwanted feelings onto others? There's little scientific reason to believe so at this time.

Chapter 6
Meditation

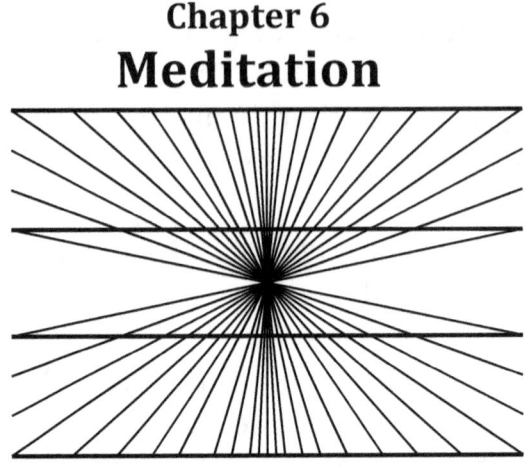

The Herring Illusion, are the inside lines parallel or curved?

Ten minutes later he was sitting in the garden, in the spaceship, once more. Obe-jo was off somewhere building integrated circuits, and Lopi, Arren's pet snake, was slithering around serenely. The brook of water trickled down the rock lined stream, like it wouldn't stop talking but had nothing important to say. Chase usually found the scene kind of calming.

But this time, it was frustratingly, *infuriatingly*, calming.

Chase breathed in again.

He and Lucky were sitting cross-legged on the ground. Arren was sitting there too, trying to lead them through something called a guided meditation.

"OK," Chase interrupted, just to have something to talk about. "Why are we doing this again?"

Space Chase: Daniel

Arren sighed, "Chase, I'm trying to help you develop your emotional intelligence[11], your ability to deal with the feelings within yourself, and in your environment."

She continued, "Through this meditation we are trying to 'reprogram' your body's unconscious beliefs. We gently try and allow your body to believe something good, instead of bad; to believe that you are safe, successful or calm. And it works, it really does work, even if the mechanism I've described is a massive oversimplification, at best. It's so successful top athletes and business executives use it. It's not a secret; it's just positive affirmations, with all their strengths and limitations."

Chase sighed, and relaxed a little. Arren seemed to know he needed the logical explanation before he'd try something as 'out there' as meditation – even if his best friend was an alien. Lucky just sat there, breathing slowly. He really seemed to enjoy meditating.

"Want to try again?" she asked.

"Yeah," Chase replied, "So what's my affirmation?"

"Just believe that you are a good person, and that you can, now and always, discern between your emotions

---

[11] A term originally made popular by author, psychologist, and science journalist Daniel Goleman in his book *"Emotional Intelligence - Why it can matter more than IQ."* The idea essentially is that knowing one's own feelings, and knowing how to respond to the feelings of others, can be more important predictors of success than simply how intelligent one is. A lively debate rages in regarding how accurate or helpful the idea of emotional intelligence is, but I notice it does get people thinking and talking.

and other people's[12], that you can, now and always, use your talents for the best and highest good of all. That's all."

"Seems pretty ambitious."

Arren smiled, "Yes, but think of it as being because the unconscious mind doesn't grasp the idea of limitations[13]. It's like a dream, everything is possible. Don't hold back. Believe it can be, and that it is right now. Then feel the power, with a touch of gratitude, of how good it would feel to achieve what you want. That's what athletes do, vividly picturing every part of the race, trying to *feel* how good it will feel when they

---

[12] This affirmation is reported as helpful by those claiming to be empaths who have difficulty distinguishing between their feelings and other people's. Some even suggest that some social anxiety phobias may be the result of unbalanced empaths, those who cannot tell between their feelings and others. Some forms of autism, where the confusion of feelings is so overwhelming an individual tries to block out everything, may also benefit from this affirmation. Again, science does not support the existence of telepathic empathy, so it's best to keep an open mind about *why* something proves to be helpful to someone else or yourself.

[13] Ahh, the unconscious mind, does it really even exist? Some research indicates, for instance, that people record the frequency of events without consciously analysing them (Hasher and Zacks, December 1984). "Automatic processing of fundamental information: the case of frequency of occurrence". American Psychology **39** (12): 1372–88. doi:10.1037/0003-066X.39.12.1372.) Indeed, we appear to tally events regardless of age, education, intelligence, or personality. But given that it's difficult to know what lies inside a mind that is unaware of itself, what can we really say the unconscious mind consists of? There is more to be learnt here, for certain.

actually compete, and when they win. Make it as *real* as possible on the inside and then, your body is programmed to make it happen.[14]"

"Worth a try." Chase muttered, still not convinced. He'd never really heard of this seemingly magical power of the unconscious mind. What was in there, anyway?[15]

"OK then, we're going to go on a journey in your imagination to the most peaceful, beautiful place you can imagine. Then we're going to imagine meeting a powerful, wise person who can help you achieve this peace, and ask them in our imagination how to find it. Their answer, inside your imagination, might surprise you. But it works, for many people.[16]"

---

[14] And such is the basis of sports psychology, see http://www.sportspsychology.net.au/index.php/coaching-coaches and Neural linguistic programing, such as http://www.inspiritive.com.au/nlp/the-new-code-of-nlp/

[15] Honestly, some psychologists challenge the very idea of an 'unconscious' mind, first proposed by Freud, that we can be thinking and feeling things we aren't aware of thinking and feeling. Some psychologists think ordinary forgetting is enough to explain repression, and ordinary denial can explain unconscious motives. Doubtless this is a complex issue that can only be highlighted in a story like this. The debate rages on, and it is a fascinating one!

[16] Wow! Lots of footnotes in this section! You might want to read on before returning for footnote goodies! But just in case, this guided meditation follows the basic pattern for many forms of meditations involving spirit guides. Science might argue it's nothing more that the personification of our own wishes, externalising our own common sense onto a 'being' that can

Chase looked over to Lucky, who was so deeply meditating it didn't even look like he had noticed they'd stopped.

He sighed. It was worth a try. Chase relaxed, and breathed in deeply. Ever since he'd realised he could feel other people's feelings it was getting harder to concentrate. Now that he knew he could manipulate them, well, that was a super power, and that needed to be harnessed properly.

Arren started talking then, telling them the same story as before. He was supposed to be walking in a beautiful meadow in his imagination. It was a very long walk, very dreary and slow. He was supposed to be crossing over a beautiful, rainbow bridge, a bridge that crossed over a tinkling river.

Suddenly, Chase felt himself become intensely aware of the little river in Arren's garden. To his amazement he could really hear it. Really. As if every plip and glop had a tiny little message to tell. It wasn't chatting inanely, it was speaking. The little river was talking mysteries with almost childlike enthusiasm.

Then his awareness shifted, and he had the distinct impression Lopi was right behind him, waving her head up and down in the air behind his back. But, somehow, Chase could feel that movement on his skin, and he wondered how. He didn't know what the snake was doing, but it felt good.

---

counsel us. But can we *really* reach animal guides or higher beings? Mainstream science at 2019 is not yet convinced.

Next, Chase felt like he became absolutely aware of everything in the indoor garden. The plants seemed alive and aware in his mind; even the stones had their place. He felt the light of the artificial sun on his skin, like it was pouring down so much more than light.

He saw, in his mind, Lucky – covered in golden light. He was surrounded by it. He saw Lopi, covered in white light. He saw Arren, and she was a little rainbow, with colours that moved like electrical wires through and around her.

He saw Obi-Jo. She was concentrating deeply, covered in deep blue light. But he also saw her pain, her frustration. He immediately felt once more how she deeply doubted her self-worth. She was not whole orangutan, but she would never be completely human. She was a freak. She would be forever.

That was when he was suddenly noticed his own self-doubt. Did anyone truly know him? His parents were never there to look after him, and so he and his brother had looked after each other. And they'd made a mess of things, so many times. Did anyone really care? It made him sick of the world and very, very … *angry*.

His eyes flew open, and he realised Arren had stopped the visualisation. "Just let it go," she told him. "Sometimes meditations bring up feelings we've wanted to pretend weren't there. If it's too much, you might like some professional help. But sometimes it's enough just to feel the feelings, notice them, and then let them go. Let them pass through, like a leaf flowing down a stream. It's not wrong to feel something; it's how we act on it that matters[17]."

Chase thought about this, but in the end, he was angry. Angry that Arren had made him feel that way. Angry that he felt that way at all. He was trying to develop superpowers, why should he feel sorry for himself?

But the anger didn't go away. It just grew.

"Huh, what?" Lucky muttered.

Chase stood up, and stormed away, "It didn't work," he muttered angrily, smashing his foot down in the little stream.

He stared away into the artificial sky, trying to calm down again. It was just a stupid thought. Just a stupid meditation. Yet now he was more angry and upset than ever, which was the exact opposite of what he was supposed to feel!

Then a strange noise arrived at his ears, and Chase turned around in surprise and indignation. It was Lucky, sitting up calmly, meditating … gently snoring.

---

[17] This is good advice for dealing with unwanted feelings, but it's not the only advice. Perhaps the best suggestion in this paragraph is 'get professional help'. It can be very important.

Chapter 7
Therapy

Duck or rabbit? An ambiguous figure.[18]

Chase looked at the sparks between his fingers.

A part of him knew it was amazing to be able to make sparks with his fingers.

The rest of him was too annoyed that sparks was *all* he could do!

Another part of him tried to tell him he was being silly, so he told it to shut up. He heard Arren sigh, probably still pitying him. It was the afternoon of the

---

[18] Why are you reading the footnotes, get back to the story guys!

next day, and they were watching TV for a school assignment, or they were supposed to be.

"I'm beginning to think you might need professional help[19]," she suddenly blurted out.

"Help?" Chase wondered, "Why?"

"Dude," Lucky said, "You're freaking out. You're freaking us out. You got these powers but they're not working out right, so you're trying to take it out on everyone else."

"I'm not ... freaking out." Chase insisted. "I'm ... freaking in."

"No, you're freaking out," Arren insisted. "Your heart rate is up over ten percent most of the time, you're short tempered and demanding. Research shows that some conditions, like depression and anxiety, are difficult for people to recognise. You need to take the advice of friends and family at those times[20]. You're freaking out Chase. You need to get some professional help."

"Oh, from who?' Chase demanded. "Some random psychologist? What am I going to say? 'Oh, I'm all worked up because my friend gave me super mind powers and I can't get them working properly.' What

---

[19] Yes, he does! But I expect Chase is going to get stubborn here. Each year, four out of every five suicides in Australia are men, perhaps, because they refused or did not know where to go for help, see https://www.beyondblue.org.au/resources/for-me/men . If your world is becoming dark or emotionless, **get help**.

[20] Get help, get help, get help.

do you think they're going to do? They'll lock me up in a white coat with long sleeves, that's what they'll do!"

"You know," Lucky seemed to be about to change the topic. "You know, the problem here is not the problem. The problem here is what you think about the problem."

"What on earth do you mean?" Chase wondered, feeling like Lucky was quoting a movie or something.

"Well, see, it's like these illusions we've been studying for the past week," Lucky explained, seeming to indulge in one of his rare philosophical moments. "How you choose to 'see' something, you know, how you chose to 'make sense of something' can make a big difference in how you react, right? It's like that picture that's either an old lady or a young lady. Now, you're looking at this and saying 'it's the old lady, there's nothing we can do about this and it's a problem.' But what we're trying to say is 'it's the young lady. Don't get so stressed, and get some help to get things fixed up.' Am I making any sense?"

"No," Chase said.

"Yes!" Arren interrupted. "Sometimes, when you see an illusion, you need someone else's help to get the fuller picture. That's what I'm saying Chase, you need some professional help to help you look into this situation properly. You are on an emotional roller coaster, and you act like you can't even tell. Plus you have empathic super powers, and are beginning to manifest electrokinesis, and you have metallic reshaping …" Her voice wandered away into a mutter, thinking to herself about something.

"Why don't you try the feds?" Lucky offered. "They ... know about us. And they've got some good people – you know they've invited me to start training with the special forces guys? At least they're a challenge, sometimes."

"No ... I didn't, you're training with them now?! I cannot believe you even *trust* them," Chase almost shouted. "Don't you remember when they threatened to *kill* you, and tried to *kill* her?" He pointed at Arren.

Arren reached over, and put her hand on his wrist. "Chase, Lucky might have a point. At least they know what is going on. Sometimes ... all it takes ... is to have someone to talk to. Even if they've *never* been through it themselves, just having someone to talk to can make all the difference."

Chase looked at Arren, and wondered what she meant. He was talking right to her, right now. *Talk to someone?*

They kept on looking at him. He groaned inside. They weren't going to leave this alone.

"OK," he surrendered, "Arren, what have you got. You're smart, you're like a professional. The meditation didn't work, what else have you got."

Arren sat back, looking concerned, "I'm not a professional, Chase. I'm not even human. I don't think I'm the kind of help you really need right now."

"You'll do," he insisted, "What you got?"

She sighed, looked over at Lucky who shrugged. "Well, we could always try Solution Focused Therapy[21]. It's pretty good with some kinds of anxiety. Many kinds of therapy, especially the older ones, focused on what was wrong. They focus on the problem, what caused it, how to deal with it. With Solution therapy you can ignore, sometimes, what started the problem. All you do is more of what works. It's a pretty simple therapy at heart."

She continued, "Say you're having trouble sleeping. Well, think about all those times you had a good night sleep. What did you do? Maybe you had a fun day, or worked out, or were too sick to play computer games. Well, just do more of that. Not getting sick, but don't play games before bedtime. Get regular exercise. Just do more of what worked. Another example, maybe closer to your condition, Chase. Say you're suffering from stress and anxiety. Well, think for a moment about all those times when you *weren't* feeling stress and anxiety, when you were feeling the opposite, say, relaxed and happy. What do you do when you're feeling relaxed and happy?"

"I, well. Reading, I like reading. Then I put the book down and have to face reality again. I don't like that."

---

[21] Personally, perhaps my favourite kind of psychotherapy - SFBT is future-focused, goal-directed, and focuses on solutions, rather than on the problems that brought clients to seek therapy. It was developed in the 1970's, see http://www.solutionfocused.net/what-is-solution-focused-therapy.

"See, you went right from focusing on what worked, to focusing on what didn't. That's not solution focused. You know, I'm *really* not doing this complex form of psychotherapy much justice[22]. Are you sure you don't need some professional help?"

Chase ignored her, "So, focus on what works. I'm calm and happy after I wake up after a nap. Naps might work, Dad seems to like them. I'm happy when I do good on an assignment, I'll admit. So don't worry about worries, just do more of what works?"

"Yeah ..." Arren said, leaning away suspiciously as if there was more she wanted to say, but wasn't sure if he was even going to listen right now. "It's just as simple as that ..."

"Great!" Chase said, jumping up, "Then I'm going to go for a walk. I always like that!"

"Chase, I – " Arren began to say, but he was already out the door.

***

The next day was amazing. Chase felt so good; he was on top of the world. Simply deciding to focus on being happy and doing what worked seemed to have made an almost magical difference in his life, and he wondered if it was that way for everyone[23].

Everything was going brilliantly. Class was fun, everyone was organised and listened to the teacher,

---

[22] No, she isn't, but perhaps I've piqued your curiosity?
[23] No. But it can help.

who made perfect sense. Chase had to laugh as he walked home, Arren and Lucky plodding along behind him. They'd been royal sticks-in-the-mud all day, but Chase didn't care. They'd been the only ones to not laugh when he'd made the whole class laugh after he'd 'accidentally' dropped the class manuals.

They'd been ignoring all the fun all day.

He turned back to look at them now, watching him, suspicion written all over their faces as he skipped and danced with the first real happiness he'd felt in days. It was only just beginning to annoy him when they suddenly stopped, their expressions turning to looks of concern and panic.

Lucky dropped his bag. Arren began to reach into one of her pockets.

And then it dawned on Chase that there was something behind him. Slowly, he turned around.

And standing right there, having stepped from another dimension or something, was the second assassin robot. Chase realised the Coebri sense of aesthetics seemed far cruder than the Universal Unity. This robot was all function, no form. It was three meters tall, with six legs and six arms. It had eyes all over its robot head, and a huge, armoured chest. And in each hand a deadly looking weapon spun, hummed or glowed.

"Another one?" Chase said, indignantly. He was ignoring the robot spilling its spiel about how Arren was supposed to come with it and 'great pain' awaited any who stood in its way. "How do they keep getting past your scanners, Arren?" he asked, jabbing a thumb back towards the robot.

"Ahh, I don't know. Might be new technology or something. Chase, I don't suppose you'd mind stepping away from the robot? I just don't want you to get hurt."

"Hurt? What, me?" Chase laughed as he suddenly realised something he realised he should have remember long ago. "It's not going to hurt me, it's Coebri, remember?"

"Chase, I don't think –" Arren started to say, then squealed as six robot arms swivelled around to point their machinations of mayhem right at his face.

Looks like I'm dealing with this myself! Chase thought, and at his mental command Random became a psychokinetic headband once more.

"Hey robot, I've got something for you!" Chase grinned and reaching up he grabbed the robot by its head, not even thinking about how he'd managed to reach up so high. He grabbed the machine by its face and, sure enough, it didn't vaporise him. Hurting him just wasn't in its programming. He grabbed it and concentrating with all his might, shot every spark his hands could produce right into the robot's head.

The sparks were dramatic, and the machine flung its arms around wildly. It took two steps back and began to smoke. Something seemed to have caught fire inside its head. It tried to raise a gun towards Arren, but Chase simply stood in the way.

Jerking and spluttering the machine slowly died.

Suddenly, a white laser shot it, vaporising it in seconds. Chase looked up, and saw Arren's spaceship hiding in another dimension destroying the robot instead of capturing it.

She explained, "They expected me to try and recycle it. It was a trap. I can't keep this robot assassin."

"They're getting smarter," Lucky said, his voice grim.

Chase was dancing, "See that? Vwoosh! Zapped it in the head!"

"Chase," Lucky said, still looking concerned, "That was only because this robot was programmed not to harm you. You've seen what the Coebri are capable of. You might not be so lucky next time."

It made Chase feel angry again. Did they not see what had just happened? Did they not care that he'd just been *useful*!

"Fine! Whatever," Chase admitted, and marched home.

All good feelings – gone.

Chapter 8
Misery Loves Company

The love of recognising form when there is none – especially faces!

The next three days were insufferable. Chase couldn't even bring himself to go to school, knowing he'd just bring everyone down. His dad didn't seem to mind. He seemed to be the only one immune to Chase's negative moods. He didn't even seem to mind how Chase could light the stove with his fingers now, only getting burnt once. His dad just seemed to take the whole world in his stride.

But by day three it was getting worse, and Chase knew he needed to try something new. Nothing was working, and every happy thought was chased out by a bad one the next instant.

Space Chase: Daniel

He was waiting for Lucky and Arren when they came home from school.

Something about his look must have scared them, because Arren paused a moment before continuing to walk. Lucky, on the other hand, was a riot of first fear, then annoyance, and finally pity. But Chase ignored that.

"Hey Chase," Arren said in her usual, confident tone. He wished he knew what she was feeling.

"What you got for me this time?" he asked.

She paused at the door.

"Are you sure you don't want to get some help?" she asked, "I'm sure the Federal Police have someone they can recommend."

"And wait for them to cut me up, like they wanted to do to you?" Chase asked, "No thanks. Not at all. No way. Just, what have you got for me?"

She sighed, and let Lucky carry her bag inside.

"Cognitive behavioural therapy[24]," she announced. "Simple once you get the hang of it. Action oriented, problem focused stuff since nothing else seems to be working. We need to challenge the thoughts you have that are allowing you to experience these negative

---

[24] CBT traces its roots from the early beginnings of psychology, from Watson's and Rayner's studies of conditioning in 1920, to Hans Eysenck and Arnold Lazarus' development of behavioural therapy techniques based on classical conditioning. It strives to solve current problems and unhelpful thinking and behaviour by challenging current thinking patterns.

feelings. Are you aware of what thoughts you have just before you begin to feel anxious or depressed?"

So it began, and went on for a good two hours. Chase slowly grew more and more frustrated. He could tell he was dealing with a rigorous, even impressive form of therapy. But talking to Arren was like taking to some kind of online psych evaluation. There was often a lack of options, and he kept feeling like she was just trying to force him into one box or another, like she wasn't trying to get to know him, she was just trying to categorise him. But then again, she wasn't a human. She was just a complex machine.

And he could tell she was becoming frustrated too.

"You're not paying attention!" she finally blurted out. "I'm trying to teach you Chase, why aren't you listening?"

He just shrugged.

She sighed.

Then there was a knock at the door.

Chase knew who it was before it was even opened. He recognised the feelings out there. It was the Federal Police.

"You brought them here, didn't you?" he accused Arren.

She shook her head, "No, it's time for the weekly meeting. Did you forget, Chase?" she asked.

He said nothing, but he was still angry.

***

Space Chase: Daniel

The Federal Police sat there, looking professional. Costa, the grim one. Flannigan, the lazy joker. And Elizabeth – the federal police woman assigned to Arren, and as luck would have it, she happened to be Lucky and Chase's mother as well.

Mum was back in her own apartment right next to where she worked in the city. Chase grinned as he remembered how she'd been spending almost all of the previous month with them coming down off illegal medicine, especially since they hadn't seen her for eight years. It was good to have her back, and good that she visited every weekend now. It answered so many questions about what he was like, and why he was so different from his dad. Chase had his mother's eyes, his mother's tendency towards order and his mother's drive for perfection. He had his dad's creativity, love of reading, and ability to waste time doing nothing.

Mum was sitting in the living room, on one of the old chairs dad had dragged up for these meetings. He sat between the two groups on a camping chair, like always. The house was actually quite respectable now, and the only scented candle to be seen was actually lit and glowing cheerily.

But Chase didn't feel cheery. He was annoyed. What topped it off, however, was that the police and his mother were shielded somehow. Chase couldn't tell how they were feeling, or rather, he could only tell what their surface feelings were. It was no more than he could tell just by looking. He couldn't get *inside* them like before.

He realised they were on to him.

"We'd like to talk to you," Elizabeth, his mother, said to Arren, "About the odd number of visitors you've experienced recently."

She sighed, "I know."

"Look, they haven't caused any problems yet!" Lucky claimed in her defence.

Costa looked grim.

Flannigan shook his head. "Look," the lanky officer stated, "Do you have any idea how far a super charged plasma beam can go before it dissipates? Those robots might not have been much trouble for you, but how much luck do you think we've had trying to cover it up for you? How do you think we explained to half a dozen residents in your area about the sudden explosions, or the small, round holes burnt into their walls and setting fire to their carpets?"

"It was a miracle no one was hurt," Mum said.

Arren cleared her throat. "Look, I'm really sorry about the trouble. But the Coebri aren't going to risk hurting anyone, are they."

"Um," Flannigan said, "That's kind of the problem."

Mum waved him to silence, "It's not, technically, the Coebri. As near as we can figure out, they're using their alliance with the Elloth to hunt you down, as a 'favour' to them."

Arren sat up, sounding disgusted, "*Those* mercenaries!"

"Indeed," Mum replied.

"Hate to be the one to sound dumb," Lucky interjected, "but, um, Elloth?"

"Giant crabs." Arren explained, "Technologically advanced, but morally reprobate. Honest, but entirely self-serving. They'd sell their own children to the highest bidder."

"They regularly do," Flannigan said, looking grim.

"This does present a problem," Arren admitted, "If the Elloth are using Coebri technology to hunt me, they are getting their hands on Coebri technology for their own ends. That could definitely upset the power balance at Kzikyah, sorry, in the Andromeda galaxy."

Mum nodded, "And all because of you, young lady."

"Hey!" Chase shouted, letting the anger get the better of him, "It's not her fault they're sending robot assassins."

The room was silent.

"Told you," Flannigan said to Costa.

Costa nodded. "A word with you, boy," he asked, politely.

Dad held his hand up, but Chase waved him aside. "I'll be fine," he told him. Besides, he wasn't to know what the most dangerous Federal Policeman on the planet wanted to say.

They left the others talking while they went outside to the front yard. Costa offered him a badge, "It'll let us talk without your friend in there hearing," he said.

"No thanks," Chase replied. He didn't care what Arren heard.

The officer looked grim, but slowly pocketed the device. "All right then. Look; get a lid on it boy. What you've got there is dangerous. We've seen the kind of abilities you're beginning to manifest before. Let's just say, you got power. But you're going to start hurting people if you're not careful. We want you to come in for some proper analysis."

"I don't think I'd like that," Chase replied.

Costa really looked grim. Chase could feel the waves of annoyance coming off him, but then again, it was Costa; he was always annoyed. "Look, whatever, boy. But you'd better rethink that. We've got robot assassins popping up that not even our best scanning devices on the planet can detect – including your alien. We've got two human boys undergoing a rapid and undetermined metamorphosis in the middle of suburbia. And now you're threatening to go nuclear? Don't you get it? We've … we've got a situation here."

Chase just looked at him. Was he worried? Was it fear? Was he afraid of losing his reputation before his superiors if he didn't keep the situation under control, or was Costa actually concerned about how innocent people might be caught up in all this?

And then Chase realised, if Costa could block his emotional reading, he might be able to transmit false emotions as well. No one had been hurt by the robots, and no one had been hurt by his growing powers. Perhaps they were all just worried, and trying to control something that wasn't even theirs. It was his, and he would learn how to deal with it in the right way, in his own time.

"Thanks, but no thanks, Costa. You worry too much. And you're waaay too angry. You could do with some psychotherapy yourself. Ease off; I don't even know why you're suddenly so 'concerned'."

Costa looked away then, away from the house and towards the city. Chase wasn't sure then; did he just talk to someone? These 'Federal Police', who were they really, and how did they have such advanced alien technology real police didn't even know about.

Then, to his surprise, Costa backed down. "All right, fine. Do it your way. Don't burn anyone and Chase, if you need it, we're here, OK! We can help you. It's not the first time."

Chase was confused, and a little incensed. Why was Costa playing 'good cop' all of a sudden? That was weird. Like he actually *really cared* about Chase. The first time they'd met, he'd threatened his Dad's life, and allowed Lucky to be thrown into a battle with a cyborg who threw cars at him. Chase was convinced – Costa was *not* the good guy.

It must have shown. Costa took a step back, and averted his eyes. He put his hands up in front of his face. "OK, OK!" he conceded, "No need to get angry boy. No need."

Chase calmed down.

"Come on," Costa said, leading the way. "Let's go inside."

But now Chase wasn't feeling angry. He was confused, and just a little afraid. *Did I just make Costa flinch? Am I really <u>that</u> <u>dangerous</u>?*

That was when Chase first began to worry.

Chapter 9
Life

Square A is exactly the same shade of grey as Square B.[25]

Life was getting confusing. And dangerous. His body was doing things it didn't use to. He was beginning to feel things he didn't use to feel. Chase was changing, and he was beginning to wonder if he really could control it.

"Control," he muttered to himself.

---

[25] Test it! Cover all but the two squares with another piece of paper - they're the same colour as each other, I promise!

Space Chase: Daniel

It was the only thing he could think about. A little bird cheeped in the early morning darkness. It was four AM, and Chase was bored of spending what felt like an entire night worrying about the direction his life was taking.

"Cats and bicycles ..." Lucky muttered in his sleep.

Chase ignored him. Throwing off his blankets in frustration he stepped over the strewn clothes and fallen school books, walked right out to the hallway and yanked on the laundry cupboard door.

It was full of laundry.

Chastising himself, he closed it and turned the handle the other way. Sure enough, it worked this time. Inside, there was the glowing white room of the entry to Arren's spaceship.

Suddenly, he heard Lucky's footsteps approach. Clearly, he'd decided he needed company, "We're going to see Arren in our pyjamas?" Lucky worried, yawning widely.

"Yep," Chase replied.

"You know, we could try asking Dad some of your questions one time. One time, just for fun?" Lucky said, checking over his chequered flannels.

"You're kidding, right?" Chase disagreed. Dad had been seen only yesterday talking to the porcelain gnomes in the garden about the health of his plants. What help was he going to be?

They waited in the brief sunbath, and Arren greeted them a moment later from the doorway. She was wearing the same outfit they'd first seen her in, and she was riding a service spider like some kind of wobbly pony. "Sup?" she said.

Lucky looked like he didn't know what to say, but Chase got right to business.

"Control," he told her. Well, demanded ... maybe.

As if the service spiders weren't useful enough - they also give free rides

She looked up, and thought. She looked like she might have even thought about saying 'Get professional help!' again, but didn't. "OK, let us take for granted that your body will do almost anything you tell it to, within the limits of its formidable capability. However, that doesn't mean it can do it right away. It takes time. Training. Understand? Losing weight, for instance, isn't as easy as changing opinions. Some changes take practice." "Right, so I'm training myself to have self-control. Got it."

"Yes. Give yourself time. It's like training a puppy."

"Training a puppy?" Chase asked.

"Yes, very much like training a puppy," Arren explained. "Treat your body like a treasured pet. It will do whatever you want, gladly, but sometimes doesn't quite get the message. So you have to be patient. Reward behaviours you want, ignore behaviours you don't want. In time, you'll begin to see the changes you want."

"Really?" Chase asked.

"Yes, it's based on operant conditioning[26]. So fun. It started with Classical conditioning, when a scientist named Pavlov was experimenting with salivation in dogs. He soon realised that his dogs began to salivate when he got out the food, even before the smell had reached them. They'd learnt to associate certain sights and sounds with incoming food. He even taught them to salivate at the sound of a bell![27]"

---

[26] This is good advice for life, but I don't know if you'd want to base your life on operant conditioning without professional help!

[27] And a whole lot more! Classical and operant conditioning are used in many kinds of fields and all over the world for different reasons. The basis of modern pet training, still, is

"How does that help?" Lucky asked.

"Training yourself," Arren explained. "If you want to achieve something, learn to associate it with good things. Reward yourself, and associate something *good* with the things you want to do or be. People do it all the time without even realising it, like when you promise yourself time off once you achieve all your work. When you keep that promise, you are rewarding yourself. That's good."

"Classical conditioning. Reward good behaviour," Chase repeated.

"And give yourself *time*. It takes time to learn to adapt to new behaviours, just like a puppy takes time to learn new skills. Say you're giving up junk food, that's a kind of punishment to the body. So replace it with something good, some reward for your sacrifice. Keep the puppy happy, and change will follow."

"What about punishment?" Lucky asked, "You know, smacking the puppy when it plays up."

"A lot of research has been done on conditioning," Arren said, "And what kinds of reward schedules produce the strongest response. Punishment is one of the least effective methods of conditioning. It does not produce strong change, usually, and it only lasts as long as the threat of punishment can be maintained[28].

---

generally based on conditioning practices first experimented with by a Russian biologist in the 1890's.

[28] According to the American Psychologist, B.F. Skinner, whose famous work on the behaviour of rats in his 'Skinner box' taught us all sorts of interesting things, punishment does not

Space Chase: Daniel

Positive reinforcement is much more effective, but here's a challenge: Which kind of positive reinforcement do you think is most effective, rewarded every time, rewarded every second time, or rewarded completely at random."

"I think I'd prefer every time," Lucky said.

"Then you'd stop working so hard for the reward, if you know it always worked." Chase said.

"Right, Chase," Arren agreed, "So believe it or not, the most effective reward schedule is random[29]. And can you think of something that rewards you at random?"

"Um, everything?"

"Just about. Even crime pays off at a gamble, and some people get addicted to the thrill even though they can be punished as well. But one that I'm really thinking about is *gambling*. For example, those poker machines. They have bright lights and happy sounds, and are made to look in every way very fun and exciting. Then they reward you *completely at random* for giving them money. And everyone knows you can't statistically make more money than you put in. But I assure you, those machines are designed to train you to put more and more money in. They train your brain!" she said, pointing to her head.

---

extinguish an undesirable behaviour; rather, it suppresses that behaviour only while the punishing agent is present.

[29] Sadly, yes. This was Skinner again, who learned this (among other things) by training pigeons to peck a button for food, and rewarding them either regularly, or irregularly. The random, irregular rewarding schedule resulted in a far more determined and pecking pigeon!

"I don't gamble," Lucky said. "On machines, that is."

"Just an interesting point on gambling," Arren told them.

"So if I want to develop self-control, I just have to reward myself, at random, for the things I'm trying to do right."

"More or less," she said. "And give yourself *time* to change. Like a treasured pet. Take it easy."

"Right, will do," Chase said, and walked right out.

"I'm not sure he understands that at all," he heard Lucky mutter.

***

Right, control. Chase had a bag of peppermint lollies in his pocket. He had a rubber band tied to his wrist.

Then, every time he exhibited good control, he would reward himself with sugar, at random. And if he was losing control, he'd slap that rubber band right down on his wrist. Nothing like rewards *and* punishment to keep things motivated[30].

And by lunch time, he was so full of peppermint he was agitated. Full of sugar, and not at all hungry. He found his thoughts racing, and he seemed to be having trouble focusing. His wrist stung from all the times he'd wacked himself, from the time he'd felt sad about Kassie's misspelling "They're" instead of "There", to the

---

[30] This is a terrible and inevitably flawed way to approach conditioning and change. Please don't try it!

time the teacher looked a little upset and he'd decided it was his own fault. Slap!

Then the teacher, who hadn't seemed to notice his strange behaviour, accidentally wrote 1970 instead of 1770 as the date Captain Cook had discovered Australia.

"Sir!" Chase shouted. "You got the date wrong."

Hang on, that was calling out in class. Slap.

"Oh, so I did," the teacher said. "Thank you, Chase."

Oh, helping the class. Pop.

Hang on, Chase realised. *People don't like show offs.* Slap.

Hang on, the teacher liked it. Pop.

Slap.

What? thought Chase. *Why did I just slap myself? Oh, it was because I was forgetting to reward myself at random.* Slap again.

But it's good to remember my training! Pop.

Suddenly his thoughts began to crash together, a random jumble so fast he didn't even have time to register them all. Pop. Slap. Pop.

"Aaargh!" he cried out, standing up, holding his throbbing head.

"Now what's *he* skitzing out for?" Mark T jeered, always the willing narrator about what was happening in the class.

Chase whirled around, glaring at him.

He felt the static electricity curing around his fingers. He suddenly had a vision of doing to Mark T's head exactly what he'd done to the robot.

Chase ran out of the room.

***

Arren found him, five minutes later, just sitting on the oval. The rubber band was off, snapped in two. The peppermints were thrown away into the grass.

She handed him his real lunch, and they just sat there, saying nothing, the whole hour.

He knew he'd overdone it, and tried to make everything change in just one day. It was a crazy thing to do.

He sat there, and ate slowly.

Chapter 10
The Lightning

A Kanizsa triangle – how many triangles are there in this pic?[31]

The next day Chase was sitting, feeling sorry for himself, in Arren's indoor garden.

He was losing it. There was no denying it now. He was beginning to feel that whatever was happening just had to run its course, and he had to stay calm and

---

[31] Actually, none, it's an optical illusion that illustrates the perceptual principal of closure!

ride out his little personal storm. At least here, in the garden, there weren't any people who could get hurt.

"And that," Arren suddenly said, "is one of the most powerful mental health techniques of all."

"What?" he said.

"Distraction," she replied, seeming to read his thoughts. "Keep busy. When all else fails don't worry about whatever is stressing you out. Just keep busy."

"But that doesn't make problems go away," he said.

"No, you still need to deal with problems. But when unwanted emotions *are* your problem, it can really be one of the best ways to deal with them. Stop focusing on it. It's like a toddler, refusing to let go of a new toy. You don't need to rip it out of their hands. You just distract them with something more interesting. They'll drop it and move on. Same thing with grownups who are obsessing... at times. Don't obsess about it. Go do something else *less painful*! And if you need to come back to it, do so with a clear mind. Take a nap, have a drink, go play golf! Distraction is a powerful way to deal with dark or obsessive thoughts."

"Hmm, thanks," he said, just glad he could sit around and not let anything bother him for a few hours. He needed a time out!

"Even so," Arren muttered, "I think you might already be beyond the point where professional help was just an option."

It annoyed him that she was always suggesting he needed professional help. But he noticed that she still didn't *make* him get help.

He knew she'd wait till he got that help himself[32].

Chase looked around at her little, calming garden. There was a movement off to the left, and a little orange orangutan walked by. She gave a monkey wave hello, and wandered on, not a care in the world.

"Arren, what is your story?" Chase asked.

"My story isn't done yet," she replied with a smile.

"I know," he said.

She sighed, and sat down next to him. "OK. This is sure to distract you! Chase: I was built over seven hundred years ago. At that time I worked for a man, helping turn asteroids into useful things. It was good work. Then one day a prospector came along. Now I think about it, it was probably a spy for my 'father' lord Tzaarkh. He came along looking for class twos such as myself for purchase. He discovered that I had an unusually high 'light ratio' – the highest ever recorded actually. You see, in order to make a soul, so to speak … the process is just too complicated to explain, but a residual of that process is a kind of, um, energy that humans can use to help them adapt. Needless to say, class two vessels are pretty popular among the Coebri. But my light was … unique. It was what we call 'resonate'. You might use the word 'perfect'. They tried desperately to buy me off him, but he refused, and let

---

[32] And that, it seems, is a sad truth about almost every emotional condition. If you are in a bad way, please get help. And if you know someone who is having trouble, please offer help. But in the end, it's almost entirely up to the individual to find the help themselves – and they can. You will find your world is full of people, friends and professionals, who are willing to help.

me tell you I was happy with that! Then one day my first owner just up and changes his mind ... or so I thought. Now I know I was just a gamble he lost!"

She looked down, seeming upset at that. "So I went to work for Tzaarkh, not really happy about it, but not really minding either. And Tzaarkh, oh, I wish I'd been a little wiser. He starts treating me like a princess. He treated me like a daughter, *better* than his own daughter! I was ignorant, but he kept hinting that I should create a Humaniform Empathy Device. A highly advanced robot form. This form here, me, with toes and fingers. This machine you relate to and call Arren. But a machine that can *experience* things almost the same as a human. He made it sound so fun. He made it sound like it would make him so happy. So ... of course, I did. I should show you the process one day. We start out as toddlers, and grow up our bodies from there, every few days growing just a little bit more. But there is a side effect of the creation of a Humaniform Empathy Device – the light becomes harvestable. We became able to transfer the residual energy from our creation ... to humans."

She looked at her hand, as though it was part of the story she wasn't quite telling. But she continued anyway. "Naturally, he never stopped talking about how *proud* he would be, how *nice* it would be if I shared my light with him. I was very young, I didn't know any better, and he was so *ill* at the time. So sick. So I gave him the red light. It made an immediate difference, and I knew right away that I'd made a mistake. Everything changed from that day. He became demanding, oppressive. Sometimes he'd pretend to be nice again, but by then I knew. He didn't care about me at all; he never did. All he wanted was what I could give him."

She stopped, and for a moment Chase wondered if she was going to burst into tears. But she didn't, and when she spoke her voice was steady. "So I refused to share my light any more. He went on to become virtually immortal, full of power and success and health. And I, well, after ten years of threats and tricks and begging ... he finally realised I was never going to share my gifts with him. So he banished me out to mine the Kuiper[33] belts with the class four monsters. It was cold, and dark and lonely. They hated me, and the Coebri hated me because of what I'd refused to do for my 'father'."

She fell silent.

"He meant everything to me," she whispered as a tear ran down her cheek. "Till I realised he only wanted me for what I had to give."

Chase waited in silence, and felt terribly sorry for her. To lose a father was one thing. To discover your father figure was only being nice to you because he saw you as a tool ... that would be a million times worse.

"That was two years ago. I waited every moment for a chance to escape. They were usually very careful, the Coebri. They knew I wouldn't escape if one of them

---

[33] Ice asteroids at the edge of a solar system. Pluto is known as the first of the known Kuiper belt objects. Eris is the heaviest. There are thousands, if not millions of cold, icy rocks out there, so far away the sun just looks like a bright star.

were on board. Then one day, I don't know. There was this half a millionth of a second where there was no one around. I never expected it, but as soon as it happened, I was out!" She laughed, "I didn't close the doors or tie down the cranes or anything. That was why there was such a fireball when I missed my landing, burning up in my rush to get through the atmosphere. Just, whoosh! Hello Earth! The only place I thought they'd never look to find me … the only place … where I thought I could never cause more trouble than I already had."

Chase looked at her as she tossed little pebbles into her river. He felt so sorry for her, and even if he couldn't feel anything she told him she felt, he believed her.

He tossed another pebble in the river for her. "Well. I'm glad you came here," he told her, honestly.

He watched then as Obe-jo wandered past. She grabbed a stick, and ran it through the puddle. She drew a line in the dirt then, running it along the ground till it reached the edge of the river. Chase watched with absent minded boredom as the water naturally flowed along the little trench she'd just playfully made.

Something about that trench seemed to absorb his attention. It was if he was drawn to it with abject fascination. It was trying to tell him something …

Where the trench went, the water would naturally, easily, simply flow.

And electricity could flow as well, from one place to another.

Just like lightning.

Chase picked up Random, and looked out then at the beautiful garden. It was full of life, and life was full of matter. And matter was full of electricity. He looked out, imagining the air full of energy, full of an infinite number of crisscrossing passages where the electricity was constantly flowing. Without forcing anything at all, he simple drew a line in the air between his hand and a faraway stone, and watched as the little tiny passages of electricity lined up along the line his imagination drew.

Suddenly a bolt of blue electricity leapt from his hand and blasted into the rock, shards of it flying in all directions. Obe-jo screamed and looked at him in panic.

Chase stared at his hand, breathing heavily.

Arren looked at him in surprise. "Woohoo!!" she squealed, "You did it, you did it Chase!"

Chase reached out his hand again. It barely took two seconds this time. The lightning cracked and sizzled into the rock for almost as long as he wanted it to, until his hand grew too hot. This time he really felt it. He felt the electricity rise up again through his feet so that he never, ever for a moment, ran out of it. Even after he was done, it still flowed into him until he remained in perfect balance once more.

This is invigorating! Truly empowering, he thought.

Bolt after bolt shot out towards the ceiling, while Arren squealed in joy. Obe-jo was nowhere to be seen.

And Chase ignored Lucky, standing by the exit, saying absolutely nothing. He turned and left, his face scowling with concern.

Chapter 11
Robots

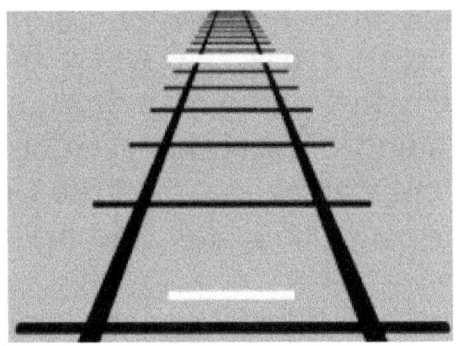

Ponzo illusion – which bright line appears longer?[34]

It was a cold Saturday, but Chase was feeling immensely better. "See, no problem now!" he announced to Arren as soon as he'd finished throwing lightning around. He tried to be like the Emperor from Star wars, but it was impossible to keep that much lightning going for more than an instant.

She smiled. "That's good. We all need a good day once in a while. But please don't think a good day means your problems are all solved, Chase, you still need to practice meditation and –"

He rolled his eyes at her. Clearly she wasn't thinking straight. Everything *was* better, as far as he could see.

She shook her head. "I'm glad you're feeling better," she admitted again.

---

[34] *Context again!*

"So, what's on the agenda for today! Blasting alien robot assassins perhaps?"

"Actually, I was going to spend the day trying to find an illusion to win me that prize! I've got a few things to show you, and … what are you looking at me like that for?"

Chase must have been staring at her again. He shook his head. "I'm sorry, I'm just not used to this whole you're not really a human thing. You look so human, then you go and fly across the universe like it's nothing. You're amazing, you know that."

"Why, thank you, Chase."

"So what I don't get is why you keep hanging out with me. With me and Lucky I mean."

She paused, "I like helping out. This life gives me so much more purpose than blasting asteroids."

"That I can well imagine."

By this time they'd run into Lucky. He was in the living room, and Random jumped down to play with him, as they so often did.

"Be a … red train!"

Random flustered for a moment as a tiny black whirlwind, then collapsed together to form a small model train replica.

It was pretty genius, Chase thought.

"Two seconds, new record!" Lucky complimented him.

"Lucky," Arren said in her teacher voice, "You realise he had to surf over seven thousand web pages, text recognise, and translate them until he found what you wanted? Two seconds is a little more than amazing, I think."

"Cool!" Lucky said, as though he wasn't really listening anyway.

"What you doing?" Chase asked.

"Just helping Random discover a few new moves, that's all. He's really fun, you should try it."

"Oh, I don't know. I don't know if we should be messing with Arren's self-aware tools, you know."

"He's not mine," Arren corrected. "He is yours, Chase."

"And he's not a tool, he's a pet!" Lucky picked the train up, "Be a triceratops again," he whispered, and Random immediately complied. Lucky sat there, stroking a small, live, purring triceratops, "Good little Random. You likes a good pet, doesn'ts you?"

Chase rolled his eyes.

Arren smiled at him, "Random is class 4 remember. He's alive, like a pet. And he'll talk to you, too, when he's in headband mode. That's what I made him for."

Chase still marvelled at it all, and realised he still wasn't interacting with Random much. Perhaps a part of him felt this was all too special for a guy like him to own? Or perhaps he was just glad Random seemed to help him think clearer? Or, perhaps, it was just like Lucky said, he was treating him like a tool, and not like a little … 'pet'.

"Hey, Arren," Lucky suddenly asked, "What's a 'class 2' or 'class 4' thingy anyway?"

Arren looked like she was feeling a little awkward. "Well, one day, in about a thousand years, if you follow traditional cultural development lines, you earthlings are finally going to figure out how to develop actual, real, artificial sentience. Not just 'self-aware' computers, but living ones. OK? Just take my word for it that computers can be aware. Now, the first discovery of sentience is what we Coebri call the class 5s. Give yourselves another hundred years, and you'll increase the intelligence, capability, and ability to express themselves so dramatically it will become, legitimately, a whole new class of sentience. We call that 'class 4'."

"So, I guess you class 2s are pretty advanced then? Did you ever get to making class 1s?" Chase asked.

"Hang on, too many questions." Arren grinned. "They make class 1s all the time, but the difference between classes 1 and 2 is miniscule compared to class 4 and 5. Miniscule, but noticeable. The differences get less and less as you get along, till class 1 is theoretically the highest possible, *almost* equivalent to human levels of sentience, I might add. But I'm a lot smarter than most class twos actually – smarter than many class 1s as well!"

"Ohh, impressive. And what level is Random?" Lucky asked.

"Four," Chase and Arren said at the same time, which made her laugh.

"Four? No way, he's a two, just like Arren, aren't you, my overly clever little –"

And on he went. "No, he's …" But Chase gave up correcting his irreverent brother. He probably didn't really believe Random was anywhere *near* Arren's abilities, but just wanted to tease them about it, because Lucky was like that.

Chase was about to launch, again, into the story of how Random could help him throw lightning now, when the mobile phone rang.

It was his mother.

She did not sound happy, and, as was her way, didn't bother with pleasantries but went right on talking as though they were already in the middle of a conversation. "Chase, I know your friend is listening to this. That last episode with the second assassin is the last straw. The government spokesperson on alien affairs is calling for an immediate transfer, while the military is demanding we post armoured tanks in civilian areas to deal with interdimensional threats. Listen to me carefully, Arren, we don't get a second chance at this. I've stalled talks for now but I don't see an immediate solution unless you find a way to detect and neutralise said threats before they happen."

"That's a lot harder than it sounds," Arren's voice said over the phone, while she stood there unmoving right next to him. "I've got every detector I know of and have invented several more. I can't figure out how they'd be slipping into the earth dimension. But give me time."

"Time is a luxury we can no longer afford, young one. Let me make this perfectly clear – should one more assassin robot or robots appear on this world, steps will be taken. You will be moved to a safer place, with or without your human friends. We cannot afford to disrupt public peace or *safety* any further."

"Yes, but don't you think it would be better just to, you know … let things sort themselves out naturally?" Arren said with a carefree tone.

"You're beginning to sound like my husband," her voice was dry and taciturn. "Actual intervention is necessary. I cannot hold off the politicians any longer. If there is so much as ONE more breach of earth's sovereign space, you will be moved."

Chapter 12
The Third Assassin

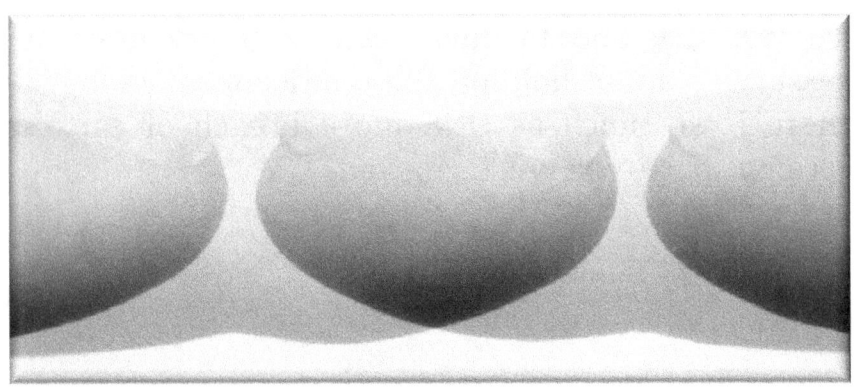

The floating finger

*Look at a faraway point
Point your fingers (pointer on both hands)
Cross them across your field of vision – but stay focused on the **far away** point, **not** at your fingers.
If you have two good working eyes, you will see a third, floating finger – fuzzy and out of focus, with two fingernails, floating in the air between your hands…*

And the third assassin was impossible to ignore.

The bell was ringing for lunch break to begin the next day, and immediately Chase recognised the welling up of anxiety in his chest. One look told the others what he already knew – the next assassin was about to arrive.

"Where?" Arren asked him, seeming to know he knew before he'd even told her.

"I can't tell."

"Let's get to the oval," Lucky said. "Get the action away from here."

"You don't think he'd really cause such a commotion, do you?" Arren asked. "It's not 'Coebri'. They like keeping the earth rule that no one here knows about their presence."

But Chase's new awareness was tingling like fire, "Well, they're about to break that rule." He was angry now. This could mean Arren would have to leave, and that was simply ... unacceptable.

"Hey, thought, bro," Lucky said. "Reckon you can get everyone away from the oval?"

Chase smiled; he knew he could.

They ducked around a corner, and Random jumped up and onto his head.

Ready for battle, master! The little robot thought to him right away.

He felt the clarity immediately, the presence of every mind in the school, even further. The gentle murmur of their different thoughts, the simple desires of their conscious minds, the kaleidoscopic patterns of their desires.

It was easy. He didn't even try, didn't even push at all. He just put the thought in there, and people almost seemed to do all the hard work for him. Without a second guess, in most cases, people simply decided to vacate the area between them and the oval, even though it was school lunchbreak.

"I wonder if they even know?" Lucky said in wonder as people started walking past them, not at all seeming bothered by the sudden exodus of students from half the school area.

"Let's go," Arren said, and suddenly a large object materialised on her arm. Chase realised her ship had just handed her one of the largest guns he'd ever seen. It was like something out of a science fiction movie, with glowing lights and weird containers. It looked like it would be dangerous in every dimension imaginable, and several dimensions that weren't.

Lucky ripped up an iron fence pole that really shouldn't have been lying around a high school, and they went out towards the oval.

They were just getting onto the tennis courts when Lucky, who was in lead, suddenly stopped.

"It's here," he announced.

They looked around. Then Chase could feel it too, an evil humming sound coming from the ground.

"Move!" Lucky roared at the last second, just as the ground exploded under their feet. He jumped clear, and Arren rolled aside. Chase, without even thinking, levitated himself far away. Eight enormous pillars of steel and stone, the claws of some mechanical being, began to pull themselves from the once smooth surface of the tennis court. They made a terrible mess, destroying it entirely. Following them emerged a huge machine; shifting and horrifying, covered with insect-like scales and with several glowing multifaceted eyes. It screamed so loudly it was a wonder people didn't come running.

Blue blasts of energy shot into the beast, but only the first two got through before it developed some kind of resistance. Chase looked to see Arren firing, desperately trying to reconfigure her device while attacking at the same time.

A massive pillar of stone and steel swung up to stab her. Chase knew she'd probably dodge it, but there was always the chance it would guess which direction she was going to move, and that was a risk he wasn't willing to take.

Everything suddenly seemed to slow down, almost as if time itself was being polite. He saw the little courses of electricity in the air, noticed them running all through the schoolhouses, the assassin, and the claw. He saw just where they were supposed to be, and just where they weren't …

And leisurely he raised two fingers, and sent an enormous white bolt of electricity right into the creature's raised limb. As the thunder struck the school, time snapped back to normal. The white lightning travelled from his outstretched hand, thirty or so meters through the air, raced up the monster's arm, and plunged deep down into the largest of its segmented limbs. With an explosion that shattered all the nearby windows the arm blasted off, showering Arren in sparks.

Chase nodded with glee, and was too proud of himself to notice the monster until it was too late. It was staring right at him.

It charged, and in that moment, he panicked. He ran.

"Lucky, get it distracted!" Arren might have shouted.

Chase tried to run away, but suddenly found his only exit blocked as the machine threw an enormous spike of stone into the ground. It could have impaled him. He tried to run in the other direction, but it stabbed the wall with one massive, clawed fist.

He looked up at its iridescent green eyes.

Then Chase looked further up and saw Lucky was on its head, and with a stabbing motion, punctured one of its eyes. It screeched as though it was in pain, a twisting tentacle on its head swung about and caught Lucky on the leg. Another bashed him on the side, and he fell twenty meters to the ground.

"No!" Chase screamed.

Before he could react red energy blasted the beast in the head. For a moment it shuddered from the blow, but instead of defending itself, it oddly raised its abdomen. Chase could see Arren then, blasting away, trying to destroy it.

The massive assassin insect robot's butt changed form then, into some kind of enormous cannon.

Arren noticed it too, and looked surprised, then horrified. She didn't even get the chance to take a breath before the machine blasted a pulse into the air, flying away in all directions. It wasn't directed at her, but the weird energy blast struck something that was invisible, floating in the air at the other side of the school. It was her ship, and it faded away again the next instant.

Arren fell to the ground. It had found a way to stop her.

And Lucky was unconscious.

Space Chase: Daniel

Chase realised he was alone.

The Third Assassin

The machine turned to face him, seeming to size him up. It seemed to be talking to someone.

Then it appeared to make up its mind. It opened its enormous steel pincers wide.

Steel, thought Chase.

He knew what to do about steel.

An instant later those enormous pincers snapped out with impossible speed and closed around him.

So, thought Chase, *The Coebri really are up to murdering us, if they can get their Elloth robots to do it for them.*

It was pretty low.

A cowardly excuse.

Just like the cowardly Coebri.

An instant later the pincers opened up, and the machine seemed momentarily confused. It studied its own pincers; seemingly curious about the life sized Chase silhouette he'd left inside the steel when he'd psychokinetically reshaped the metal around himself.

But it didn't think about it for long, and struck again. And again. But each time he just readjusted the metal.

By the fifth time he'd had enough. He grabbed the pincers and refused to let them close, deforming them at the creature's mouth. The massive assassin seemed to struggle in his grasp. He spoke to all the metal in the monster, and told the steel in its legs to weaken. There was a sickening crack, and with a shout of triumph Chase threw the monster away. It stumbled backwards, struggling to stand up.

But it didn't take long to recover. It opened its mouth, and prepared to spew something all over him.

Chase had had enough. He was disgusted. He was *angry*. How did they think they could get away with breaking yet another of their own rules? Why would the Coebri send such a pathetic, easy, weak challenge to test him? Why did they think they could ever challenge the heroes of earth?!

The mouth opened wide, but Chase just laughed. Pressing his hands together he just made a motion as if he was pulling the monster apart. He didn't have to touch the metal to manipulate it this time. It simply moved wherever he told it to.

It sounded like a car wrecker's yard. The metal screeched like he was torturing the beast somehow, but Chase just kept laughing. Within a few seconds he'd torn a hole clean through the monster and right out the other end.

It fell to the ground with such a thunderous crash the whole school shuddered.

Chase laughed.

He looked around then, and noticed several people looking.

Oh, he told them, *Nothing you want to see here. Move on.*

They did. They all did. Some simply forgot they were looking. Some were terrified, and pressed the memory out of their minds immediately. But they all went away.

Chase felt it before he saw it. Arren's ship had recovered, and it was approaching. It floated somewhere over the tennis court and began to take away the assassin into whatever dimension it usually was.

And by the time it was gone Arren and Lucky stood side by side.

She did not look pleased.

"Impressive, brother," Lucky complimented him.

What's your problem? Chase asked Arren through the headband.

She looked down, then at Lucky, before she replied. *You shouldn't be able to do that yet. You just shouldn't. That was too advanced.*

Chase was incensed. *What, am I too impressive for you now?! Taking away all your glory from winning?*

No! It's not that, not like that at all!

"Then what is it!" Chase shouted.

Random slithered off his head and became a watch again.

"It's," Arren said, looking at Lucky again. "You need, um, energy to do what you just did. That was several tonnes of thorium enhanced titanium. You shouldn't have just done that with your own emotional power[35]."

"Well, I did!" Chase almost shouted. "Why … and why can't you just be happy that I did!"

"Hey, chill guys!" Lucky said.

"I am!" Arren said, holding her hands up in a 'calm down' kind of gesture. "I am, Chase. Thank you. Thanks for defeating that assassin robot. I don't know how we would have done it without you."

Chase smiled.

Yeah. That was more like it, thought Chase. *Now I have some **real** power!*

He didn't even hear himself laughing.

---

[35] Using negative emotions to power telekinesis is science fiction, but emotions do affect every decision we make. Every wondered what it might be like to have no emotions at all? Not so great, I assure you!

Chapter 13
Class Goes Wild

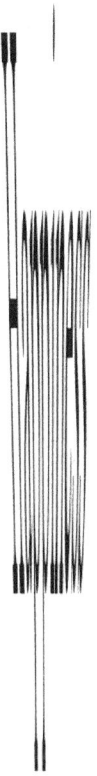

Sometimes what really matters is how you look at things. Potential chaos can make complete sense from a different point of view. Look at the above image from a steep angle.

A different point of view

Feelings. Emotions everywhere.

Everywhere.

Even animals had feelings.

And feelings were something he could control.

And emotions were something that could make him powerful.

And the world was full of feelings!

Chase sat there, revelling in a school full of feelings. He felt them all, from the overly concerned principal, to the distracted, yet honestly affectionate janitor everyone ignored.

Everyone had *feelings*.

But a part of him, a part he was trying to ignore, realised that Arren had stopped talking to him, and Lucky was too nervous to try.

So the day passed in a silent whirlwind of emotion. He didn't even notice the thirty or so children who went into the sick bay with emotional disturbances, or care that they closed the school early to call in a biohazard team to try and figure out what was going on at school.

But he was very well aware that the Federal Police were waiting at home.

Chase walked in calmly. Everyone else was already there, even Arren and Lucky. Everyone was nervous. They were all on edge. So when Costa finally spoke it was like a dam bursting.

"We've had enough!" he yelled, louder than even he expected. "It's just. These *machines*. They keep attacking. We've got in over our heads with a meteorite hitting a school, the newspapers are all over it! I've just … this is crazy."

"Don't talk to my kids like you own them!" Dad shouted.

"Darryl!" Mum burst out.

"It's all right, Mum," Lucky said.

"Don't talk down to me, young man!" she said.

"I'm lucky if you talk to me at all!" he shouted.

Then Costa shouted. Then Dad some more. Even Arren got into it.

Everyone, except Flannigan. He just looked right at Chase, and seemed to think, *You had enough yet?*

Chase stood up, and asked everyone to be quiet without speaking a word. They shut up immediately.

"I'm going to fix this now," Chase said, calmly.

Everyone just looked at each other, not seeming to know what to do.

Chase held up his wrist, where Random sat obediently pretending to be a watch.

Arren's eyes grew wide with fright.

Chase told Random to become the headband, and he did. Immediately the room felt colder, but Chase hardly noticed.

"Chase, what are you …?"

He silenced her with a glance. Flannigan was reaching for his glasses, while Costa just seemed unable to move, his eyes staring at the headband.

"I'm going to fix this now," Chase repeated. He walked towards the door. It was just another barrier. Or was it? Maybe it was just dust too?

It had disintegrated before he'd even touched it.

Mum screamed, or she might not have, it was difficult for Chase to tell in the thunder of emotions that rolled through his head. Everywhere, people had feelings. And feelings had power.

He reached up, and floated through the air. The next thing he knew he appeared on the school roof, near the windmill tower.

For a brief moment he wondered why he was here. Then he remembered. He was going to fix things. He wasn't going to let them take Arren away again. He was going to find out how the robots kept finding them, and why they could never seem to find the robots.

He reached out then. He felt Random squeaking in protest, but he just ignored him. He was a tool, after all.

Chase reached out and grabbed the metal windmill. Suddenly it was as if he could see into nearby dimensions. It was so unbelievably easy, once he believed he could.

And sure enough, he found them. Instantly. There were ten of them, large floating balls of metals and stone, looking like alien, space-aged satellites. They were in positions all around the suburb.

There was a sudden flick of light, and they shifted dimensions. But Chase had no trouble finding them again. It was the flick of light; another small machine, not much bigger than a pencil.

It was another class five machine.

Random spoke: *Master, the other class five is controlling the satellites. If you want to stop them, you'll have to stop the little light first.*

Space Chase: Daniel

Alien spy orbs!

Matter was easy to control here, so Chase just reached out his hand and made the little light fly towards him. Suddenly the strange orbs began to surround him, a half dozen more appearing from across the world. They drew out sharp knives and snapping lasers to threaten him.

He turned them inside out without a second thought. They crashed through to the normal dimension, bits and pieces of them smashed to the ground, scattering like metal rain.

Now the other class five had nowhere to go. Chase reached out, and snatched it in his hand.

It was a clear crystal, long, white, and very fragile.

Suddenly Random pressed a thought into his mind. *And, Master Chase, it is alive.*

Chase paused. Was he really about to smash this device? Yes, actually he was. Hmm. Maybe he still should? But then he thought about Arren. She was alive too.

So, Chase asked it instead, using Random's help. *How did you hide from Arren?*

It trembled mentally at his power. *I am sorry, Master! They made me do this!*

How did you hide! he demanded.

They didn't think she would look in the near dimensions. They are carefully warded by Earth's guardians. They were right, of course. Until you looked here, Master. Please, have mercy!

Mercy? You almost got her thrown off our planet. You almost got me killed! How am I supposed to show you mercy?

Please, I'm just a machine. You … you don't … you don't realise, do you? The only way we could have existed here was …

He paused.

Random filled the silence for him … *if they were invited.*

What? Chase roared.

Please, don't hurt me! I don't know. I just work for the Elloth. They sent me here and told me to watch for when she was not looking. Then they sent in the assassin bots. They don't have feelings you know: the perfect assassins. Not like me … eh? it begged.

Invited? Chase mused. *Who … who! Who invited you?!*

Ahh, I don't know. We only call him the Caretaker! He's the one you want! He's the one working with the Coebri to try and get unit Arrendrallendriania away! Please, please let me go.

Chase had had enough. He was not about to let this little, evil crystal go.

It was just obeying orders. Random pleaded.

Chase's hand began to close over the fragile, crystal machine.

Then a thought struck him. So, a puppet master? A man behind the curtain who was really pulling the strings?

Your life is mine now. Chase told it. *And you're going to go back to the Elloth and tell them I found you. That way, they don't go thinking it was just an accident. Tell them we know what they're up to, and we aren't happy. Tell them to get out of their alliance with the Coebri and off our world or we will deal with them personally. I am sure they don't want an angry human and class 2 vessel looking around for answers.*

No, sir! Yes, sir! The machine begged, *Oh, thank you, sir! I will tell them immediately.*

And don't come back without my permission, do you hear?

No, sir! Not without your personal permission, sir!

And with that, it was gone.

For a moment there was silence. Chase was only vaguely aware of the wind that wrapped around him. There was no one to be seen in the school. Leaves and dust bounced around in the gale below him.

So. A puppet master. Chase wondered. *A 'caretaker'. Someone with the authority to invite aliens to earth?*

Who could it be?

He reached out then, reaching out with his mind. Looking for someone, looking at all the people. But instead he just found normal people. Normal people, with normal problems.

But there was a lot of people.

A LOT of people.

And they all had feelings, and feelings were power.

He reached out, further and further. He didn't even notice the wind raging around him.

"Chase, stop!" A voice called to him.

He looked down. It was Arren. "Chase, calm down. You can't do this all on your own!"

"Yes, I can!" he shouted back. "I found out why we couldn't stop the assassins. I took care of this. Now I'm going to find out who invited them!

"Chase!' Lucky roared. "Stop it, stop it now! Look at what you're doing! You're going to hurt someone!"

Finally, he did look. He saw the weather he was causing. Somehow, channelling all that negative emotion was also causing a terrible storm.

And in that very moment, he was able to let it go.

The wind died, and Chase found himself clinging to a windmill over ten meters high. With a cry of surprise and fright, he grabbed the metal with both hands. He must have been levitating or something. Random became the watch once more.

He could almost feel Random's indignity at him destroying the other probes.

I'm sorry, I'm so sorry, Random, Chase apologised.

Random said nothing.

Mum and the others waited till he climbed down, Costa leaping up to assist him.

When he got down, everyone looked at him with concern. He stuttered out the story and everything he'd just learnt as quickly as he could.

"That's important information, thank you," Mum said, "And I, for one, am glad to see how you dealt with the probes so effectively. But what was with that cyclone?"

"It's ... just ... there are so many feelings!" Chase admitted.

"Channelling emotional energy is dangerous work. What is sent out is immediately replaced, you know," Flannigan explained, and heaven only knew how he knew that. "You can end up on a kind of feedback loop, you know, creating more and more of what you're trying to get rid of? Creates ... disturbances."

"Come on, Chase," Arren said. "Let's get you somewhere that's famous for not having your kind of problems."

"That might be a good idea," Mum nodded.

Chase jumped up, glad to escape the judgemental attitudes. He, Lucky and Arren all hopped inside her space ship.

Chapter 14
Nariou

It ... moves...

"It's the Cambrianian word for 'peace'," Arren explained. "They found it ages ago. Or re-found it, no one I've spoken to have records that go that far back."

Chase looked out in wonder. It certainly was the kind of place that took your breath away. He was in the indoor garden, but the outer door was open and they were standing on a floating platform high above in the air.

And outside, there was another world. Or to be more precise, another dimension. Lightning danced on indigo clouds to the depths of a red horizon that appeared to have no end. Silver and pearlescent orbs moved between them as though purposeful, and alive; though what matter of being or cause that moved them was an enigma. The orbs moved and swam together, making new shapes and geometrical forms as though they were part of an infinite calculator whose purpose could only be guessed at.

It was calm, and serene, and utterly sterile. There was no life, no real being. To Chase it was like a painting; a highly artificial reality.

And it was boring.

"Take me home," he asked.

Arren nodded, seeming sad, but she didn't obey him. "Don't you like it here?"

He found himself fidgeting. "It's too quiet," he confessed.

"After your spate on the windmill I would have thought you'd like a place without many emotions," Lucky told him.

"But this isn't peace. This is *nothing*. Peace is at least something. But I see why you brought me here Arren. You think you can help me sort out my feelings without hurting anybody, because there aren't any feelings around here at all."

"Well, I did hope," she said.

"Then I guess we came to the wrong place. There's nothing here to be sorted out, except me. And Lucky, he's nuts too. But maybe this is just what I need. To get all the feelings out. To become as sterile and feelingless as this place is. Then at least no one will get hurt."

"You can't destroy feelings, Chase. They're a part of you, and they belong to you. They tell you important things, even if they're not always helpful, or seem very accurate. They're a part of being human, a part of what makes you so powerful. Don't try and kill your feelings, Chase[36]. You can't stop feeling despair, unless you also never feel hope again. It's just all so precious. You can't stop being afraid without losing the ability to love. Don't take that away. Don't … become a machine," her soft voice begged.

Chase stopped, looking out at the noiseless beauty.

"Then what do I do?" he asked. "What do I do when I feel things I don't want to feel?"

Lucky answered. "You've just got to get through it, buddy. Just hang in there. You'll handle it. Weather the storm."

"And talk to someone!" Arren begged, "Someone you can trust. Several people at once if there's no *one* individual you think you can trust. Get on the Kids Helpline! Just … talk."

Chase nodded. It had been an intense day. He'd been drowning in a storm of emotions. He'd taken on all this emotion … now it was time to get it all out.

"I could use some peace," Chase thought out loud.

"Yeah," Arren agreed. "Do peace."

They came home, but Chase wasn't feeling peace.

He wanted to get to work.

---

[36] That really is good advice. Some psychologists believe feelings never go away until they are resolved. They will just wait around until you are ready and if you ignore them for too long, they begin to surface without your permission. Feelings tell us important things.

Space Chase: Daniel

***

By the time Chase came to himself again, he was already standing on the school roof. The wind whipped around him, tiny dots of rain finding their way down from the sky and onto his skin.

But he didn't care. Random was a headband again, but Chase didn't even check to see what he thought about that.

Nariou was nice, but it was boring. Even so, it had given him an idea. Earth was too noisy. It was *too* emotional. If he could take all that away, sort out all the feelings, then maybe he could move on.

He would force peace on earth.

But first, he had to deal with all the feelings.

He had to weather the storm.

***

Lucky knew there would be a problem. So Lucky did what Lucky does when there are problems he can't handle personally. He played computer.

He heard Arren talking to his mother even while the storm outside got wilder and wilder.

"He didn't even say goodbye. He just teleported away as soon as we got back. I don't know how he was able to do that, even with all I've given him!" Arren told them.

"What is happening?" his mother demanded.

"As far as I can tell, he's attempting to transfer emotional energy to the weather, trying to dissipate it!

But it doesn't work like that! He's only going to make things worse!"

"Then you've got to stop him!" Mum shouted.

"We'll try. Come on Lucky!" Arren shouted. "We've got to save Chase!

Lucky looked at the rapidly darkening sky.

But who will save us from Chase? he wondered.

***

Arren whisked them inside her space ship to the foot of the school.

Lucky looked up at the roof, "Couldn't get us any closer?"

"There's a lot more than wind to be worried about now," was her cryptic reply.

Chase was nowhere to be seen. But up in the darkening sky a cyclone was forming right above the school and without looking Lucky knew that his twin brother would be right in the eye of that storm.

"Gosh, all I did was break a few sheets of glass and a couple of footballs. Why does he get to break the weather?" Lucky asked, indignant.

Arren turned to him, her face written with concern. "This isn't the time for your humour, Lucky. Chase is in real danger. He's making it worse. He needs to get out of this storm before he levels the entire city."

Lucky looked at her, this strange best-friend-of-his-brother. Ok, call it as you see it; this weird, not-quite-girlfriend of his brother from outer space, who was now personally responsible for giving his brother superhuman mind powers that were about to blow up the city.

"This is the perfect time for humour! Come on, space girl. Let's get up there and fix your mistakes."

"I... oh!" she shouted in frustration above the cyclonic winds. He heard her following him inside. Suddenly the far windows burst apart, and a powerful wind tore through the school, the wind seeming to fight them every step of the way. Arren dragged him to the side, and pushing away the dust and debris they made their way to the stairs. Arren tried the handle, but it broke off in her hand.

"Chase!" she protested, "let us help you!"

The doors stood shut.

"You really think he can hear - " Lucky began.

"I know he can," she interrupted.

Lucky bent down, summoned his energy and smashed his foot against the door just the way the secret service guys had taught him. They'd actually been teaching him quite a lot since he'd started training with them, but Chase still hadn't asked him about it and he wasn't about to tell him either.

The door splintered in two. It was as if the metal edges had welded themselves tighter, and he had to break it right away from the wood. Fortunately, that was something he was quite capable of doing. They raced up the stairs, the wind howling outside.

Suddenly, Lucky stopped. He turned around, because he thought he heard someone running up the corridor behind them. Yes, now he thought about it, it sounded exactly like someone young and very heavy running up the corridor, against the wind.

But there was no one to be seen.

Lucky ran to join Arren at the top of the stairs.

"Once we get out there," Arren tried to say, "we're going to have to help him calm down. Don't say anything stupid, ok?"

"What? Me?" Lucky managed a grin. He didn't want her to know, but right now, he was terrified for his brother. He'd never seen anything like this, except in movies.

And in the movies there was never the very real chance that someone he cared about could actually get hurt. Chase was lucky – he always had Lucky to take care of him. But what would Lucky do if Chase was going to destroy himself? Could he really just let him? He knew, right there and then, that he'd never, ever forgive himself if that happened.

He hauled at the doors, and they popped open with such surprising ease he almost fell over except for his superhuman reflexes.

And there, standing silhouetted in the drenching rain, was Mark T, a massive crowbar clutched in his hands.

Chapter 15
Confrontation

Lucky just stood there, unable to comprehend what was happening.

"I don't know what you're doing!" Mark T shouted in the rain, "But I'm here to stop it, for good!"

Lucky got his bearings, and laughed, "What, with that?"

Mark T hefted the large iron weapon. "If necessary. Look. I don't know what you did to Chase, Arren, but it's going to destroy the school if we don't shut it down. And I'm here to shut it down."

Lucky laughed, and looked over at Arren.

But only so he'd have enough of a distraction to grab the weapon off Mark T. He lunged forward and twisted it around so that Mark's wrist would be turned painfully the wrong way. He was just beginning to think how clever he was when Mark stabbed him with what must have been a home-made cattle prod.

It was as if he'd expected Lucky to grab the crowbar the whole time.

Electricity shot painfully through Lucky, knocking him to his knees and stealing away his breath entirely. He heard Arren scream, a kind of angry scream that sounded like she was about to break her apparent pledge of non-violence against humans. Lucky tried to move his arm, but it just didn't seem to want to obey him right now.

"There, how's that feel, *Lucky*!" Mark T scoffed.

Lucky saw Arren move quickly, and decided to help her keep her pledge. Sweeping his leg around he managed to take Mark's feet out from under him. With a cry of surprise Mark fell sideways and whacked the side of his head on the concrete. Lucky tried to stand but found he couldn't; it seemed kicking Mark may have just broken his ankle.

To his surprise, Mark stopped fighting. He just sat up, and clutched his head, and whispered, "You idiot!"

Again Lucky tried to stand, but couldn't.

"Get out of our way, Mark," Arren demanded. "You have no idea what is happening here. No one can stop Chase but himself, so there's no way an iron bar will do it."

She slipped her hands under Lucky, who put one arm around her and they began to walk away.

Mark T rolled over, clearly in no condition to battle further. No power on earth, it seemed, could stop him from talking. "Don't I?" he demanded, clutching his head. "You think I don't remember who you are? Or those pirates you used to work for? I don't know what you did to Lucky and Chase, *Arren*. But I'm going to stop it. Somehow. I'm going ... I'm going to save the world."

Arren stopped.

"Then *save* it," she insisted, and left him lying in the rain. "By leaving us alone."

Lucky leant on her heavily as they hobbled on towards Chase. The howling wind intensified, and soon they had to crawl. Lucky thought he could hear voices in that wind, but shook his head. There just couldn't be voices in the wind.

They found Chase kneeling by the air conditioning units on top of the school. The wind twisted in his clothes, but the air above was sky blue. It was almost surreal.

Suddenly, there was a beep, like a mobile phone ringing. Arren looked surprised, and reaching down pulled out a little phone. She looked at the screen.

"It's your mother!" she told Lucky.

Lucky wasn't sure what to think. "Why would she be calling at a time like this?" he shouted.

Arren gave him a 'what do you think' look, and handed him the phone.

"Hi, mum!" he said, trying to sound cheerful,

"What is going on?" she demanded. "We can't get satellite imagery of the location. The Americans are going crazy, they've demanded we scramble the F1-17's. We need answers Lucky!"

"Well …" Lucky said, not too sure of what to say. He looked out at his brother causing raw, primeval chaos, "I don't know what to tell you, really. Nice day we're having, bit breezy though. We're having loads of fun, but Chase seems to be about to destroy the world."

"What? Get through to him! Hurry Lucky! We need a solution."

"Yeah, working on it."

"Give Chase the phone, immediately!" she demanded.

Good luck with that, Lucky thought. He reached out finding his leg quite paralysed. Perhaps it was the electricity? Stupid Mark, it made him wish he'd aimed for a little more than a bumped head.

Arren grabbed the phone, putting it on loud speaker though he wasn't sure how that'd help with the wind howling against them.

"Chase, it's your mother-"

She didn't finish.

A black dust began to swirl around their feet.

"Oh no," Arren gasped. "What has he *done*?!"

The black dust suddenly grew, seeming to come from everywhere, forming a strange beast-like shape with a whirlwind for a tail. It stood above Chase, defending him, roaring in the wind.

"Random?" Lucky pondered.

A second later the huge monster tore the air conditioning unit off in a single move and shredded it into two with its silicate claws. With a terrifying roar to rival the cyclone above, it threw the remains off the school and onto the ground.

The black dust continued to swirl, smashing everything until the nearby roof was entirely swept clear of any debris, or places to hide.

The dust looked up, and screeched; a horrifying noise like every fear and hatred of humanity was combined into one terrifying sound.

Lucky found himself shaking.

"Chase, what have you done?" Arren whispered.

She was crying.

The Monster Random swept out at them with a claw of dashing winds. The phone was snatched from her grip, and before their very eyes, crushed to pieces.

"So much for that," Lucky said, then noticed how Arren's hand was cut and gently bleeding.

That wasn't like Chase at all.

That was when Lucky, in spite of every hope in his heart, sincerely began to wonder if this would end well.

"Chase! You have to-" he begun, but Random roared up at him, blocking out the sunlight.

Suddenly there was a terrible crash, and Lucky didn't need to see what had just happened. The Gym had caved in. The multi-million dollar school gym was no more.

How far was Chase going to go? he wondered.

"Right," Arren stated.

Lucky felt, rather than saw, the massive form that was her spaceship suddenly appear in the air.

"You need to stop this!" Arren shouted, standing up. "You need to stop this now, Chase! And if you will not stop it, I will stop you!"

The trees at the front of the school began smashing, one by one.

Lucky turned around to see the spaceship high in the air. Next to him Arren began to glow with her nuclear heat.

The ground trembled. "Now earthquakes?" Lucky wondered. And suddenly he got the distinct, and undeniable, impression that this battle, if it happened, would never go well for anyone.

There would be no winner.

"Mark T!" Arren suddenly screamed. She stopped glowing in an instant.

Lucky saw him, on the other side of Chase. Mark T was standing at the edge of the vortex. He was unarmed.

Random floated through the air to menace him.

"Mark T, get back!" Arren roared, her voice coming from everywhere.

"NO!" Mark roared. "This is *my* world, remember? We solve our problems right here, right now. All of us, remember?" He was quoting words he'd heard her speak in class.

She floated back to the ground, but her eyes still glowed.

Lucky couldn't even stand. But he could shout, "Get back, you idiot!" He was feeling very dizzy right now. "Can't you see this is beyond you?"

Mark T looked up, right at Random. It was clear from the look in his eyes that he was terrified. He had never seen anything like this in the movies either.

But like Mark T was going to let something like that stop him.

He took a step forwards, and Random roared. He raised a massive scythed fist towards the boy.

Lightning glowed in the sky from Arren's spaceship.

"Stay out of this!" Mark screamed at Arren, and took another step forwards.

Random raised his hand.

"He won't hurt me!" Mark insisted. "This is Chase we're talking about. We just need to talk, Chase. There's something I want to tell you!"

"Mark, get out of there!" Lucky shouted.

Random tensed. Arren screamed.

Mark took another step.
And Random struck downwards.

Chapter 16
End

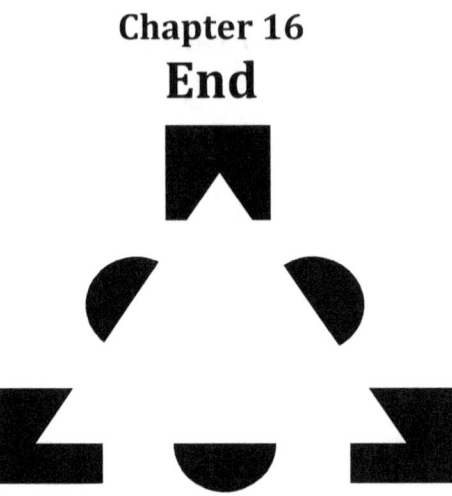

The principle of closure. How many triangles are in this figure?[37]

... and Random stayed there, hovering millimetres from Mark's head.

Random growled, but didn't stop Mark from walking towards Chase now.

He got to within two paces of the kneeling boy, and never before did Lucky wish more that he had a crowbar to throw at someone, just in case.

"Chase," Mark shouted, "Chase, listen!!!"

***

Chase was listening. That was the problem. He had finally discovered that there were some things so

---

[37] None! Your imagination is able to 'close' up the figure to create a triangle that isn't there ☺

engaging, so passionate, it was impossible *not* to listen. He wasn't on an emotional rollercoaster; he was on an emotional freefall. Gravity had taken over, and he was going down and down and down.

And there was nothing he could do about it.

Dustbeast

So when he looked up, and saw Mark T standing there, it was no surprise. What did surprise him was the lack of violence or hatred in the big bully. He was honestly just ... trying to help.

"Chase!" Mark T repeated. "Listen. You need to get off this roof!"

That annoyed him, and the lightning showed it. The wind tore at the school, and at what was left of the trees. He heard more of them break, and that only seemed to add to his satisfaction. But every moment of destruction only pointed to the endless amount of suffering, fear and regret in the world. Feelings that needed to be dealt with. Feelings that could be dealt with if he just smashed enough things to be done with it...

... until tomorrow. When new feelings would be born, and new problems would be created. Humanity was like that, always making problems for itself.

But Chase only seemed to be able to deal with everything right now. Tomorrow didn't exist. If he could make everyone forget their feelings for one day, he might never have to worry about tomorrow.

Mark T looked at him. For a moment he didn't say anything. Then he huffed. "You need to go see your Dad," he said in an almost conversational tone.

Trees broke.

"No, I'm serious Chase. I don't know what's got you going like this. I know you could kill me standing here but you won't. I don't know what's going on. But I know you need to talk to your Dad. OK? So, you just gotta trust me. Go see your Dad."

Chase looked up, confused. This was the great bully's solution? He looked over at Arren. She begged him with her eyes. He looked over at Lucky, and found him lying on the ground looking just as confused as he was.

Lying?

Was Lucky hurt or something?

The storm suddenly slowed, and Random fell into a shower of sand.

"Lucky?" Chase asked.

"Come on, brother. Mark is right, for *once*." He stood up, but seemed to need Arren's help. "Ignore me. Just go see Dad."

Chase didn't know what to think, his feelings were still crowded out by world-wide angst. It was a lot to process.

More than any human should.

"Yes," thought Chase out loud, though it seemed difficult to turn thoughts into word right now. "OK then, I will go see Dad."

The next instant he found himself, standing, in the garden back at home. The place was filled with a fierce wind that threatened to knock over every plant and building there. But it quickly died as soon as Chase arrived, thunder still rumbling in the sky.

"Chase!" A voice called out.

It was his Dad.

Before he could move the old man had wrapped his arms around him. "I'm so glad to see you," Dad said, his voice choked with emotion.

The storm broke. Suddenly the chaos of emotions fell silent, and Chase felt peace in his father's affection. The wind died, and a gentle rain began to fall.

"Ah, what good luck!" Dad said, holding him with one arm while admiring the rain, "I was so hoping it was going to rain!"

Chase had to laugh. Dad didn't even seem to be aware that it was he that had caused the rain, and that it might not have stopped till it had flooded the entire city.

But one look in his hazel eyes dispelled all myths. Dad knew. Dad knew perfectly.

"Dad …" Chase asked, not sure of where to begin.

"I know son, I know," he said. He hugged him again, and Chase couldn't help but start crying.

It had been a big week.

"I know." Dad said again.

"Dad…" Chase repeated, trying to find the words to explain what was happening. But he couldn't. There just weren't any.

"You know, son. I don't know if this is going to help, but I'd like to say it anyway. When I was young, I used to play soccer."

"Soccer? You want to talk soccer at a time this?"

Dad just smiled, and continued, "Well, one time I was selected as forward for the under eight team. Not that I was very good, everyone got a turn. Anyway. We didn't score a single goal that day, but there was this one time, son. This one time where I was ahead of the group. I was heading for the goal. Then I noticed how many legs there were. Then some woman screams 'Go for it, mate'! Then I started feeling unsure. Then I kicked."

"And?" Chase asked, enjoying tales in the rain.

"And I missed. Naturally."

"That's your story?"

"That's my story! Yes. But not the lesson. You see son, I was worried about too much. I was trying to deal with everything. But the only thing I should have worried about was getting that ball into that goal. I should have just concentrated on that one thing. That's my advice."

Chase wondered how that helped.

"You don't have to deal with every problem in the world, son. You only need to make sure you do the right thing with the responsibilities you've actually, currently, got."

He thought about it.

"You know, there's world-wide pollution, and corruption, and all that. But you don't need to fix *all that*. You only need to make sure you do the right thing with what you've been given. If everyone remembered to be honest, and take care of the things they were responsible for, it would fix just about all the problems in the world. The rest of the world will take care of itself, eventually. That's what I believe."

Chase felt frustrated again, "But I can make a big difference in this world."

"Yes, you can, and you do. But you don't have to worry about problems you haven't been given. If you become a teacher, then worry about teaching well. If you become a businessman, then you worry about honest business. If you become a fireman, then you worry about putting out fires. But don't take it *all* on son, it's not yours to take on. People... gotta learn to solve their own problems or they just keep getting back into the same situations. You can't fix everything for them *all*. You make a big difference by just being here, so enjoy it."

Chase stopped.

It just seemed to make perfect sense. His dad was right and had somehow seen through him. What was it about a parent's words that could get through when no one else's made sense, that helped him change the way he felt in spite of every professional he'd met, or scientific psychotherapy Arren had told him about?

Dad bent down, and began pulling weeds. "Son, you're just a kid, for now. So worry about kid things, Daniel."

"What did you call me?" Chase asked.

"Daniel. Your true name. I've been saving it for an occasion just like this, when I needed to speak directly to you. You see, there's an old shamanic theory -"

"You're so weird!" Chase protested, and with a laugh, bent down into the dirt, and helped his father clean the muddy, soggy garden.

Chapter 17
Daniel

Can you find your blind spot?
Cover your right eye, stare at the circle, and move the book slowly backwards or forwards until the star disappears.

"Daniel," Chase announced. "Though I still prefer Chase. We'll keep it for special occasions."

They were at the school the next day, helping to clean up. School was cancelled for the week, but still just about everyone was there helping where they could. When the SES people would allow them, that is. Arren was sweeping, and Lucky was picking up huge stones and throwing them in a bin.

"Daniel?" Lucky muttered. "That's not fair! I wonder what my real name is?"

"Daniel!" Arren smiled. "That's such a nice name. It is Hebrew, you know."

Chase smiled, but his smile covered an enormous amount of shame. In spite of every good intention of his heart, his desire to take on too much of the world's problems had almost caused a catastrophe. The mere fact that he'd done it was almost enough to drive him crazy. But he didn't give himself time to go insane. He was too busy cleaning up the mess, beginning with one unswept corridor at a time.

He looked over and saw Mark T among those helping to clean up, a bandage on the right side of his head.

Lucky stopped working to stand beside Chase. "I think someone must have knocked him to the ground." He smirked, a vivid picture of what had happened replaying in his surface thoughts.

Chase smiled, he couldn't help it, Lucky's was so contagious.

Arren spoke up, "Hey, leave off. That boy helped save the world yesterday – or at least to save *you*."

Chase nodded, and tried to say thank you to Mark. But he was not paying any attention, and maybe that was a good thing.

His two lackeys came up to help Mark T.

"He's told them too, now," Chase read in their surface thoughts. "They're calling themselves the 'Homeworld Vigilantes'."

Lucky laughed, "Better than the 'Planetary Sell-out-to-the-Coebri'."

"Guess he's not completely the bad guy," Arren seemed to suggest to them as though only thinking out loud to herself.

Chase pondered, unsure. He could feel that there was still a lot of trouble inside that young bully, even if he had somehow managed to find his way through all that to help Chase find his own peace. "Maybe!" he muttered.

Yet he didn't like the thought that two other guys knew about Arren now. But he felt even less comfortable about trying to erase their memories or something. They'd just have to deal with it when they came to it.

"How was this morning?" Arren suddenly asked him.

Chase sighed, and kept sweeping up rubble. "OK, I guess. They got a psychologist from Fiji, of all places. Said she's had experience 'with this kind of thing'. She was pretty good, I guess. I didn't tell her much, but she's got these funky meditations I'd like to try. Might be good."

"So, you think you'll be all right?" Arren asked, looking concerned.

Chase was about to answer when Lucky interrupted, "Yeah, no more destroying the world with natural disasters, OK?"

Chase smiled. "Yeah. Back to dealing with my own problems. Like that stupid illusion competition!"

Looking past Arren to focus on Lucky, Chase suddenly realised something amazing. He saw two Arrens. Each of his eyes saw a different picture, superimposed on the background. It was as if there were two illusionary Arrens standing, smiling at him.

And he had a very clever idea.

***

Next week they were back in class, meeting in a windy and hot undercover area since the science room still wasn't officially ready.

It was the day of the illusion contest. There were some great entries. Kassie had drawn a huge poster of a really detailed illusion that looked like a tree or two people talking, depending on how you looked at it. Everyone was very impressed, some even murmuring she'd gotten some help, but Chase knew she hadn't.

Then it was Chase's turn.

He stood up proudly, "I call this the eleventh finger trick. The illusion doesn't even need any drawings. Look, if I hold my hand up in front of my face and point my finger, see, it looks like I have two fingers! So since I now have two pointer fingers on my right hand, I officially must have eleven fingers!"

He was so proud of his accomplishment, he didn't even notice anyone trying it out. He turned to the teacher, who didn't really seem impressed.

"That's nice, Chase."

"I already knew that," Kassie protested.

No one was impressed.

Chase was aghast – he was sure he had the winning entry, the illusion that didn't even need a picture! Mark T glowered at him, grinning, but too cunning to insult him right now.

He huffed, and sat down.

Stupid competition, he thought to himself, careful not to dump those feelings onto anyone else.

"Well, we've seen some pretty impressive illusions today. I believe we only have two more entries? Mark."

The bandage was off, and Mark T walked up to the front of the room with his creation under a dark silk sheet. With a flourish he removed it. Underneath was a strange box covered in bright silver hologram paper, the kind you might use to cover books for school work.

"May I present to you ... the Ames Room!" he said, his voice confident and arrogant as always. Mark T was back, that was for sure. "You look through this hole in the front of the box here, but the back of the box has an illusionary wall designed to trick your senses! The normal cues for depth perception have been remooooved! So," and here he turned the box to face the teacher, "if you look in here, as I move this doll from one end of the box to the other, it can be perceived as the doll actually growing, and not getting closer! Look."

The teacher did look, and actually seemed impressed.

"Here," Mark T said, "Here's the maths I used to calculate the proportions of the box."

Now the teacher looked really impressed.

"Oh no," Lucky said, clearly it looked like he was about to lose his bet.

"That is perhaps the best illusion today," the teacher said, and everyone could hear an audible gasp from Kassie. "Arren, where's your illusion."

"Just a simple one, maître," she told him. "I want to help you all find your blind spot."

Arren began handing out little pieces of card the size and shape of a small bookmark. She had an amazing presentation using images from the internet. She took time explaining the science of how the nerves in the eye needed a way to get out, and that they make a spot in each eye that couldn't, actually see. It was impressive, and even though it took ten minutes, in the end everyone could find their blind spot.

Everyone was impressed, but none more than the teacher. "That's ... amazing! I've never been able to find my blind spot before. Look, it's right in front of my face! Wow!"

He carried on and on.

It was clear who would win this competition.

***

Lucky wasn't happy. "You. I can't believe you won that competition with your stupid illusion-that-isn't-even-an-illusion trick!"

It made her laugh. "Lucky, you can't win at everything!"

Lucky groaned, shaking his head. "You can't see everything either, apparently." Lucky turned and kicked a stone over to the other side of the oval and right out of sight.

They laughed.

Suddenly Arren stopped short. There, appearing in front of them, without any warning at all, was a little robot. It melted in from another dimension just like the assassins. It looked a bit like a hypercharged television on two spindly legs.

Lucky was a few steps back and too distracted to even notice, Chase and Random were holding sparks in the next.

Arren just stood there.

The little TV looked around like it was a little lost. It turned, and with an audible sigh, stated, "Oh, thank goodness I've found you!"

"At least this one talks," Chase said.

Do we smash it now? Random asked.

"I don't think that's Coebri …" Arren pondered out loud.

The TV put a pair of spindly, hinged arms on its 'hips' in a kind of indignant gesture. "I should think not! No, this isn't a Coebri issue, not at all."

"Then what is it?" Chase asked.

"You'd better come with me," the machine said, its voice gentle, almost begging.

"Trouble with the Elloth?" Lucky asked.

The TV shook its head. "Worse – trouble with the *Mechanizer*…"

Appendix

References

Three pronged widget, Techner circles, Herring illusion, Happiness, finding your blind spot. Made by Dr Joseph Ireland, 2012 sometime.

Scintillating grid illusion, taken 8th June 2015 from http://en.wikipedia.org/wiki/Grid_illusion

Pinna's illusory intertwining effect, taken 8th June 2015; http://en.wikipedia.org/wiki/Optical_illusion#/media/File:Pinna%27s_illusory_intertwining_effect.gif

Duck-rabbit illusion taken 31st March 2015 from http://en.wikipedia.org/wiki/File:Duck-Rabbit_illusion.jpg (American public domain – created before 1923)

Face among the leaves, also taken 8 December 2015 from http://www.maniacworld.com/face-in-trees-illusion.html. Original artist unattributed.

Colour contrast illusion (square A and B are the same colour) taken 8 December 2015 from https://en.wikipedia.org/wiki/Illusion#/media/File:Grey_square_optical_illusion.PNG

Kanizsa triangle taken 31st March 2015 from http://en.wikipedia.org/wiki/File:Kanizsa_triangle.svg

Ponzo illusion. Taken 31st March 2015 from http://en.wikipedia.org/wiki/File:Ponzo_illusion.gif

Illusionary motion. Taken 8th December 2015 from http://www.hdwallpapers-3d.com/cool-optical-illusions/cool-optical-illusions-wallpaper/. Original unattributed.

Space Chase: Daniel

How to count in Coebri

By Arren

Centuries ago, a highly influential philosopher and mathematician convinced the scholars of her time that the most successful counting system would be base 64. Her culture went on to conquer the known world at the time. This means that, unlike your nice sensible earth system where your numbers repeat every 10 digits (that is, zero to nine) Coebri children have to learn the exact names of the first sixty four numbers on their own. I'll write them here so you can learn them all.

	-om	-en	-ip	-off	-ia	-alla	-if	-ix
Tzall-	0	8	16	24	32	40	48	56
Thol-	1	9	17	25	33	41	49	57
Gharr-	2	10	18	26	34	42	50	58
Knar-	3	11	19	27	35	43	51	59
Smorr-	4	12	20	28	36	44	52	60
Op-	5	13	21	29	37	45	53	61
Arr-	6	14	22	30	38	46	54	62
Driarn-	7	15	23	31	39	47	55	63

So the first eight numbers are 0-Tzallom, 1-Tholom, 2-Gharrom, 3-Knarom, 4-Smorrom, 5-Arrom, 6-Opom, And 7-Driarnom

I know it looks complex, but it's actually quite simple and intuitive once you get past the basic rules. Kids use their fingers just like us, with a half extended finger for the first 4 numbers, fully extended for the other eight. The other hand (usually right) can then be used in the same way to represent the 'eights' column, and you'll be pleased to know basic arithmetic including division and multiplication can be worked out using your fingers in this system.

After the first digit was expressed, a second word might be used to represent which multiple of sixty four it represented. Just as we use 'two hundred,' the Coebri would use 'three sixtyfours and eight.'

64+	128+	256+	512+	1028+	2056+	4112+	8224+
Nor	Tal	Gor	Tzup	Talmin	Gkormin /Halron	Rrotz	Dralmin

The use of either Gkormin or Halron is cultural, and doesn't affect counting. Both are accepted.

'Nor' is therefore the same as saying 'sixty four', and 'Nor Driarnix' as 'sixtyfour and sixtythree' or 127.

'Tal' is 128, 'Tal Nor Driarnix' is 128 and 64 and 63, or 255.

3000 is 'Halron Tzup Gor Tal Tazllif' (2056+512+256+128+48), which may seem like a mouthful, but 'four thousand, one hundred and twelve' is simply 'Rrotz'. Languages are like that.

In terms of modern culture, Talmin and the further names are rarely used, and Dralmin is used to represent the highest number used by early cultures, meaning 8224.

Just as you use 'thousand, million, billion' etc., Coebri prefer now to repeat the first 512 numbers with new words to indicate amount. First we work in multiples of 512, much the same way as you go 'ten thousand', 'a hundred thousand', etc, they simply repeat the number and add a new prefix.

So;
Thollen Tzup is 9 x 512s, or 4608.
Thollen Tzup Gor Open is 9 x 512s and 256 and 13=4877
Tzallip Tzup 48 x 512s, or 24,576
Nor Tzup is 64 x 512s or 32,768
Gor Tal Nor Driarnix Tzup is 511 x 512s or 261,632
Gor Tal Nor Driarnix Tzup Gor Tal Nor Driarnix = 262,143

But what to do when you want higher numbers? What is one to do beyond Tzup Tzups? Another multiplier, of course!

Tzup	512 to 512^2-1 (start at 512 up to 262,143)
Drallen	512^2 to 512^3-1 (from 262,144)
Mirid	512^3 to 512^4-1 (from 134,217,728)
Gkoll	512^4 to 512^5-1 (from 68,719,476,736)
Xkamarr	512^5 to 512^6-1 (from 10,445,360,463,872)
Nok	512^6 to 512^7-1 (from 5,348,024,557,502,464)
Ollon	512^7 to 512^8-1 (from 2,738,188,573,441,261,568 up to 1,401,952,549,601,925,922,815)

I.e., Drallen = Tzup Tzups, or 262,144

Beyond that we begin to get into unusually large numbers, so these will suffice for the present.

There's a bit of overlap between the early and modern systems. For example, 7000 is both, 'Rotz Gkormin Tzup Gor Driarnip' and 'Open Tzup Gor Nor Tzalloff', (confusion is avoided since Talmin, Gkormin/Halron, Rrotz, and Dralmin as a prefix to Tzup never act as multipliers, just additives. You think it's confusing? Try learning it when you're six!)

Likewise, 2095 is Halron Driania or Smorrom Tzup Driarnalla.

Remember the numbers are never written with spaces, this is just convenience for learners like yourselves.

And note on pronunciation
Tz – a hard z, as in a zee with a t in front of it.
Rr – double rr, rolled as in Italian but deep throated.
Gk – a hard g, deeper in the throat that simply 'g'.
Ix – As in 'fix'.
L vs ll – l is short, ll is longer.

Thus, Arren Drallen Driarnia = $14 \times 512^2 + 39$.
It's quite a simple number, compared to some numbers, really.

About the author

Dr Joe (AKA Dr Joseph Ireland) is a science educational specialist operating out of Brisbane, Australia. He has a wife, three daughters, and a flute. He enjoys playing Dungeons & Dragons with friends and has written award winning fiction for the Living Greyhawk series. His true passion is in understanding and promoting scientific ways of thinking in society, having lectured in Science, Technology and Society at Queensland University of Technology.

If you're looking for an exciting science show for your school why not visit www.DrJoe.id.au to find out more!

Daniel is the third book in the series *Space Chase*, which explores sound scientific concepts within the framework of an engaging science fiction narrative. This story focuses on the sciences of the mind and personality, while helping a young man on the cusp of his burgeoning powers.

I LOVE SAMANTHA!

Book 4
The Mechanizer

One of Earth's oldest allies is sick – deadly sick. What can Lucky, Chase and their best friend Arren do to prevent an impending techno-apocalypse? Perhaps the mysterious Caretaker of planet Earth can provide answers, if only they knew who or where he was! Or will a sick machine bent on self-preservation overtake the entire world...

The Mechanizer is the 4th book in Dr Joe's "Space Chase" series that explore sound scientific concepts through a fun and engaging narrative. Learn about forces, motion, friction and gravity as you help Lucky, Chase, and their alien friend Arren to save the world!

Place your mark here each time you read this book!

Feedback and comments are always welcome Arren@drjoe.id.au

www.ingramcontent.com/pod-product-compliance
Lightning Source LLC
Chambersburg PA
CBHW072336300426
44109CB00042B/1646